I am inspired by food . . .

For more information or to contact the author visit her website at:
www.SimpleHealthNetwork.com
Or her food blog page at:
www.OMGAllergyFree.com

OMG! That's Allergy Free? Vol 2
Copyright © 2011 by Simple Health Network, Spokane, WA.

Library of Congress Cataloging-in-Publication Data
Parker, Peggy, ND, Biological Medicine Diplomat
ISBN 978-0-9847997-0-1

Special Diet – Recipes

Printed in the United States of America, Book Printing Revolution. First printing November 2011.

OMG! That's Allergy Free?

The ultimate gourmet guide to delicious wheat-free, dairy-free, sugar-free, gluten-free food.

RECIPES AND GENERAL TEXT

Peggy Parker, ND, Biological Medicine Diplomat

COVER DESIGN

Angela McKendree

PHOTOGRAPHS

Dr. Peggy Parker

DEDICATION

This book is dedicated to so many people . . .

To my daughter Allison who has been a willing taste tester as well as my official food critic, food trend educator and the source of much encouragement . . .

To my daughter Angela, without her technical help and advice, project management, gentle corrections, patience in teaching me proper layout skills and her beautiful cover design, this book would never have looked so good . . .

To my son Michael who taught me the necessity of either hiding veggies in everything or making them taste fantastic – these skills have been invaluable in my recipe development . . .

To my daughter-in-law Al who kept the brainstorming alive until the title appeared . . .

To my girlfriends who lent me kitchen tools, participated in my cooking experiments, made me feel at home on their couches, helped me make connections and patiently endured hours of phone conversations and countless emails while I made this journey . . .

To my patients, blog followers, Facebook fans and everyone I've met as I travel, who are dealing daily with food sensitivities or allergies . . .

You have all inspired me and I thank you . . . your help, encouragement and support mean more to me than words can express!

It's my hope that the recipes in this book will inspire you, nourish you and have your friends and family all exclaiming in delight . . . OMG! That's Allergy Free?

TABLE OF CONTENTS

INTRODUCTION

Hippocrates, the Father of Western Medicine, penned a quote that is the basis of my medical practice . . . "Let food be your medicine and medicine be your food."

As a physician of natural medicine, I understand the importance of this idea in creating more vibrant health for myself, my patients and their families. And as a former chef, I find the variety in the foods we have today absoultly inspiring . . .

However, like you, I live a busy life filled with a wide variety of ways that require my time, my focus and my discretionary spending. I also understand that not everyone has the desire or the training to create elaborate meals that take hours to prepare. When dealing with food allergies, food sensitivities as well as the decision to simply eat healthier, it's important to know what is in the dishes you are eating or serving, and how to capitalize on nutrition without sacrificing taste, texture and visual appeal. Making it even more important that the time spent in your kitchen results in food that's reliably delicious, nutritious and fun to eat and serve! With that in mind I have designed, then triple-tested every recipe to ensure your highest level of success!

To make the most of your time, energy and money, on the following pages I have provided a list of what I consider to be my top nutritional choices. By simply substituting or adding just one of the OMG! All-Star foods from each category to your diet 3-4 times a week, you will begin to build more vibrant health!

My Top 30 OMG! Nutritional All-Stars

To make your journey to delicious eating, nutritious choices and vibrant health as easy as possible I have identified my top OMG! Nutritional All-Stars in categories like grains, legumes, fruits and veggies. While there are so many wonderful and delicious choices in every category, my selections all have the distinction of having an impressive nutritional profile as well as outstanding health benefi ts, combined with great taste, low cost and availability.

Creating vibrant health is as easy as adding at least 1 item from each category to your weekly shopping list! You will be surprised with the noticable changes in your own health, energy levels and well being in only a few short weeks! And you can accomplish this while eating beautiful and delicious food!

I have made this task even easier by creating recipes that focus on dishes that include these superfoods, so you can choose a recipe from any category and know that you are adding powerful antioxidants, vitamins, minerals and fiber that will do your body good! You can use this list as a handy reference guide while making your weekly menus. Bon Appetite!

Ionized Water

While water is not technically a food, properly ionized water can be your biggest ally in the ongoing battle against oxidation. As a tireless reseacher, author and lecturer on this subject, I would be remiss if I did not mention what I believe to be the single most important source of antioxidant action we have available today.

To really understand this concept it's important to understand that oxidation is created by free radicals. It's also important to understand that oxidation is the culprit behind disease, aging and death! So while slowing down the cycle of oxidation is great, stopping it altogether is the goal! Here's a little information to help you understand the unique differences between the antioxidants found in the foods we eat and properly ionized water.

The OMG! Nutritional All-Stars all have one thing in common . . . they are rich in antioxidants. Antioxidants all have this unique property - they are all willing to donate a piece of themselves (an electron) to quench or neutralize a powerful free radical from damaging our cells and tissues. While this is vitally important, there is a down side to this action. As each antioxidant donates an electron it then becomes a weak free radical itself! The end result is that the antioxidants in foods and supplements *slow down* the cycle of oxidation to a more moderate level, but *can never stop* or even significantly slow this cycle of disease, tissue destruction, aging and death!

While this may seem dismal, there is some good news!   The antioxidants found in properly ionized water (produced exclusively via electrical current) are unique in their ability *to stop or significantly slow down* the cycle of oxidation.   Unlike antioxidants in foods, the free electrons that are produced in the ionization process have no down sides.   This is due to the fact that properly ionized water contains only free electrons that have the potential to quench any free radical period!   Free electrons never become free radicals!   This revolutionary discovery is the basis for my research.

So combining the special antioxidants in ionized water with vitamin, mineral, fiber and antioxidant, anti-inflammatory foods can help you achieve the highest levels of vibrant health!

Throughout the recipes in this cookbook I have utilized ionized water, but if you do not currently have access to it, simply replace it with clean, preferably filtered water.   If you would like more information on this topic, please visit my professional website at www.SimpleHealthNetwork.com where you will find free articles, lectures and webcasts.

Now on to the food . . .

Sweeteners

Sweeteners are a great place to make a HUGE impact in the nutritional content of your daily diet.   There are so many delicious choices on the market now and each of them has health benefits that allow you to sweeten your coffee or tea and even indulge in an occasional sweet treat without guilt!

I highly recommend, date sugar, maple sugar, light molasses, honey, stevia, palm sugar, coconut sugar and even evaporated cane juice, but the 3 OMG! Nutritional All-Stars of sweeteners are **stevia, black strap molasses and brown rice syrup!**

The sweet leaves of **stevia** plants make a zero calorie, zero carbohydrate sweetener with serious health benefits.   Green powdered stevia is a powerful anti-inflammatory proven to normalize blood sugars, restore the health of the pancreas, lower high blood pressure and even reverse gray hair and wrinkles!   For best results in baking use it in combination with brown rice syrup to produce fantastic results!   The brown rice syrup produces a similar caramelization effect of traditional sugar, while the stevia enhances the sweetness.   It's an altogether tasty pairing with fantastic health benefits!

Brown Rice Syrup is a sweetener with almost magical properties!   With little effort it transforms into delicious caramel, icings and even candies!   Because it's made from the bran of the rice kernel it is packed with the essential minerals manganese, selenium and magnesium which are essential to cellular health and a vital immune system, plus the amino acid tryptophan to help us stay calm and sleep soundly!

Black Strap Molasses is an excellent source of both B vitamins and a wide array of minerals. Made from the thickest and darkest unsulphured, minimally processed syrup from sugar cane, it contains approximately 90% of the nutrients available from the canes before it is boiled and then crystallized into sugar. It provides the distinctive flavor we love in gingerbread as well as dark rye bread, and is used the world around in baking and cooking. Even though just a little can provide a great deal of flavor, that small amount also provides a considerable nutritional boost as well! Just 2 teaspoons provide significant amounts of iron, manganese, copper, magnesium, potassium and calcium. These minerals are responsible for bone health, oxygenation of the blood, regulation of enzymes, the production of pigments in the hair, skin elasticity and elimination of toxins. It also delivers a significant amount of B vitamins – aka Happy Vitamins – to coat nerve endings, modulate mood-elevating hormones, prevent birth defects and so much more!

Flours

While spelt, kamut and faro are among the most nutritious ancient wheat varieties, most flour blends in GF cooking and baking are among the least nutritious items in your pantry. Since GF baking became a bit more popular, pastry chefs and home cooks alike have been relying mainly on starches to produce lighter and better tasting baked goods. However this is a nutritional nightmare, producing baked goods that are the nutritional equivalent of a Twinkie!

The great news is that there are a wide array of nutrient dense nuts, legumes, grains and seeds that are both naturally GF and nutritional powerhouses! So adding a bit of these to one of your favorite flour blends is a quick and easy way to turn a dessert or treat into a nutrient dense food that will actually do your body good! Among my favorite additions to both glutinous and GF flours are ground fava beans, garbanzo beans, buckwheat, brown rice bran, millet and amaranth. But for taste, texture and nutrition the 3 OMG! Nutritional All-Stars of flours are ground **oats**, **almonds** and **quinoa**.

Oats are one of the most beneficial of all cereal grains. Oats are naturally GF, but can be contaminated during harvesting or processing. So be sure to purchase certified GF oats if you are gluten intolerant. Oats are not only amazing sources for minerals like manganese, selenium, phosphorus and magnesium; they also contain significant amounts of antioxidants and fiber. In fact the antioxidant, known as avenanthraides, together with the fiber, beta glucan, are powerful protectors of our cardiovascular system. They actually work together in this way - beta glucan lowers LDL cholesterol and avenanthraides protect the LDL from oxidation resulting in a significantly lower level of plaque in blood vessels, while speeding up the transportation of infection fighting white blood cells wherever they are needed in the body!

Due to their mild flavor and fine texture when ground, **almonds** are a perfect addition to any GF baking. They "lighten" otherwise sticky starches and provide a protein substitute that's crucial in building the structure in baked goods that allows the water content to expand during baking to produce a tender, light and fluffy end product.

In addition to those important functions almonds are an excellent source for essential minerals like manganese, magnesium, copper and phosphorus, which work to build collagen and elastin in our skin, allow our blood vessels to expand and contract properly, regulate blood sugars and decrease inflammation. They also contain a generous amount of the amino acid tryptophan, which regulates sleep and creates a sense of calmness. Plus they contain heart healthy vitamin E, which has been proven to increase cardiovascular health, and riboflavin, which regulates the conversion of carbohydrates to, sugars resulting in energy production and balanced blood sugars!

While considered an ancient grain, **quinoa** is actually a seed from a plant that is closely related to spinach. This tiny seed is a storehouse of vitamins, minerals and has a complete amino acid profile! So when it's ground the proteins, like those in almonds, provide a framework or structure for baked goods. Packed with very high amounts of manganese, magnesium, iron, copper and phosphorus, it also contains significant amounts of riboflavin, tryptophan and lysine. Lysine is essential for tissue growth and repair and is generally missing from all other plant-based proteins. Based on all of its constituents, quinoa is considered a valuable addition to all diets, but especially helpful for anyone with migraine headaches, cardiovascular disease or diabetes.

Additionally, quinoa's high levels of manganese and copper boost the levels of the antioxidant superoxide dismutase (SOD), which helps to protect the mitochondria from oxidation during energy production! And its high fiber content has been linked to breast cancer prevention. It's no wonder this tiny seed has been dubbed a superfood!

Grains and Seed Grains

Whole grains and seed grains are among the most important sources for fiber, B vitamins and a wide array of minerals in our diets. While gluten containing grains must be avoided by anyone with an intolerance, there are many more naturally GF grains than gluten containing grains.

Whole grains are a vital part of meals in cultures throughout the world because they are excellent sources of the complex carbohydrates we need to produce ATP – the energy that fuels our cells. Some of the most popular whole grains and seed grains available today include buckwheat, spelt, kamut, farro, einkorn, oats, barley, wild rice, millet, rye, sorghum, teff, triticale and corn, but the 3 OMG! Nutritional All-Stars of the grain and seed grain family are brown rice, amaranth and quinoa.

Since you can find information about **brown rice and quinoa** above in the Flour section, I'm only going to address amaranth in this section. Like quinoa, amaranth is actually a seed of a nutritious leafy green that is eaten in many cultures around the world, and like quinoa it is an excellent source of vitamins, minerals, fiber and protein. Amaranth is an excellent source of manganese, magnesium, phosphorus, iron, copper, zinc and calcium as well as a whole complex of B vitamins, Vitamin K, Vitamin A and even a small amount of Vitamin C, plus it contains 15 grams of fiber and 14 grams of protein per serving! Unlike quinoa it contains only 8 of the 9 amino acids (it lacks lysine) but is still a significant source of plant based protein.

It's unusual nutritional profile makes it a strong support for cardiovascular health, its constituents are also responsible for building red blood cells while increasing their ability to transport oxygen, guarding against colon, breast and prostate cancers, increasing energy production (ATP), normalizing blood pressure and blood sugar, decreasing inflammation and increasing fat burning! Like quinoa, it's easy to see why this tiny seed is also considered a superfood!

Herbs and Spices

Herbs and spices are among the best ways to add a depth of flavor to anything you are cooking or baking! In fact skillfully utilizing them allows you to decrease other less desirable ingredients without sacrificing flavor. In addition to those powerful attributes, herbs and spices are sources of important vitamins and minerals. Natural medicine practitioners have used them for centuries. Their constituents are so powerful that they have been synthesized in labs to create nearly every drug on the market today.

So liberally using fresh and dry herbs like parsley, rosemary, thyme, cinnamon, cardamom, anise, sage, turmeric and oregano can help your body do everything from balancing blood sugars to fighting cancer and infection, to detoxifying the liver and regulating blood pressure. Of all of the amazing herbs and spices to choose from, because of their taste, versatility and healthy properties the 3 OMG! Nutritional All-Stars in this category are **basil, ginger and cayenne.**

Without **basil** no pizza, pesto or Italian sauce would ever be complete! There is no substitute for this delicious culinary herb. But you may not realize it is also a very beneficial medicinal herb as well.

From a nutritional standpoint it is extremely high in Vitamin K – the essential vitamin for proper regulation of blood clotting factors. But that's not really where most alternative medicine focuses. You see basil contains two other distinctive health-promoting factors. Its two water-soluble flavonoids – orientin and vicenin – have been shown to protect both white blood cells and DNA from oxidation. While its volatile oils are potent anti-bacterial agents that are effective even against antibiotic resistant strains! If that were not enough these oils are also more effective in blocking the COX enzymes than any over-the-counter non-steroidal anti-inflammatory medications including ibuprofen, acetaminophen and aspirin! Plus, basil oil has been demonstrated to be a potent agent for removing toxic petrochemicals from the body.

Sweet, spicy and aromatic, **ginger** is a culinary staple in Asian, Indian and Middle Eastern cooking. It's used in both sweet and savory dishes, baking, candies, teas and carbonated beverages the world over.

While you may be aware of its ability to calm a queasy stomach (that's why your Mom gave you ginger ale), you may not be aware of it's many other health benefits. Ginger has been shown to boost the immune system, increase detoxification (via sweating), induce death in ovarian cancer cells, offer protection from colorectal cancer and is a powerful anti-inflammatory agent! All this and it's a good source of potassium, magnesium, copper, manganese and Vitamin B6.

While I was in Naturopathic College I was dubbed the title of Cayenne Queen because of all of the research I did on that particular pepper! When compared to all of the health promoting properties of other herbs and spices, none can compare with the vast array found in **cayenne** pepper. While it's an excellent source for beta-carotenes and a good source of Vitamin C, manganese and Vitamin B6, its most important component is capsaicin.

Cayenne has been proven to relieve stomach ulcers, improve overall gastrointestinal issues including colon cancer, respiratory illnesses including asthma and sinusitis, relieve pain even from osteo and rheumatoid arthritis, prevent free radical damage in the circulatory system and even reverse diabetic related nerve damage, fight inflammation, boost immunity, increase metabolic action, clear congestion and even increase weight loss. But of all its properties, the one I value most highly is its ability to increase the circulation of both blood and lymphatic fluids. Since these two fluids are responsible for the delivery of oxygen and nutrients to the cells and the removal of toxins and metabolic wastes, it's easy to see why cayenne pepper is earning its reputation as the Holy Grail of healing compounds.

Nuts and Seeds

Nuts and seeds are unarguably the most nutrient dense foods we can consume. They are literally packed with minerals, including important trace minerals, vitamins, enzymes, healthy fats, fiber and protein. They are readily available, amazingly portable and ever so yummy without any cooking! A handful of nuts as a snack or added to your favorite sweet or savory dish can boost the nutritional content by leaps and bounds!

Loading up on these nutritional powerhouses is as easy as a quick trip down the bulk isle of your favorite natural foods store. Each of them has a unique profile of oils, minerals and vitamins that are unparalleled in any other food. You will find sunflower, -sesame and even poppy seeds, hazelnuts, almonds, pecans, macadamia nuts, peanuts (actually a legume), cashews, pistachios, pine nuts, Brazil nuts and more. But the 3 OMG! Nutritional All-Stars of the nuts and seeds category are **pepitas, walnuts and flax seeds.**

Pepitas or pumpkin seeds offer unique health benefits particularly for men. They have been demonstrated to promote prostate and bone health in middle aged and older men. This seems to be linked to their high levels of carotenoids, Omega-3 fatty acids and zinc. These crunchy little seeds are powerful anti-inflammatories and have been tested alongside the arthritis drug indomethacin with only 1 notable difference. While the drug has the undesirable side effect of destroying the linings of the joints, pepitas actually protect the fatty lining, slowing down the progression of arthritis.

A single salad with 2 ounces of pumpkin seeds and a dressing made with pumpkin seed oil every week can actually make a significant difference in antioxidant and anti-inflammatory levels in your body.

Walnuts have recently been the subject of a wide variety of clinical studies that have outlined some of its unique properties. They are unusually high in Omega 3 fatty acids and gamma-tocopherol (the exceptionally heart healthy form of Vitamin E), plus more than a dozen phenolic acids, tannins and flavanoids, high levels of alpha-linolenic acid (ALA), and the minerals manganese, copper, calcium, chromium, iron, potassium, selenium, vanadium and zinc, as well as melatonin! This impressive list is unique to these yummy nuts.

Here are some of the health benefits and uncommon characteristics from this unique combination of anti-inflammatories and antioxidants . . . Walnuts have been shown to lower LDL while protecting HDL cholesterol, increase cognitive memory function, regulate sleep, increase the sensitivity of insulin to balance blood sugars, prevent breast and prostate cancer, guard the cardiovascular system from oxidation (including the ability of arteries to remain elastic), lower triglycerides, enhance bone stability and stabilize weight!

Adding as few as four ounces of these OMG! All-Stars to your diet weekly can produce rather impressive results! Just be sure to refrigerate walnuts to keep their oils fresh.

While they come in tiny packages, flax seeds are very impressive! Beneath their tough exterior lies an abundance of alpha linolenic acid (ALA). ALA is then converted to Omega-3 fatty acids and Omega-3 is converted into powerful anti-inflammatories in the body. So flax seeds and flax oil are the vegetarian's best source for these powerful protectors. These fats have been proven to increase the flexibility in cell membranes, making them more receptive to minerals and hormones, including insulin. In addition to the fatty acid profile, flax seeds contain ligands that have been demonstrated to protect against the formation of blood clots, reducing the risk of strokes and heart attacks, as well as several forms of cancer. They also regulate blood pressure, lower LDL cholesterol and triglyceride levels faster than statin drugs, and stop the growth of prostate cancer.

While the majority of the studies (more than 1600) were based on ground flax seeds (grinding allows the system to utilize the oils, minerals and ligands), whole flax seeds are very effective in regulating bowel activity and toxin removal due to their fiber content. Adding 1 teaspoon of both whole and ground flax seeds to smoothies, cereal, salads and baked goods 4 times a week over a 3 month period can produce remarkable results! That makes these little powerhouses an undeniable OMG! All-Star!

Greens

A day without greens is like a month without sunshine! In the world of veggies, greens reign supreme. They are unequalled in their vitamin, mineral and fiber contents. In fact one cup of greens has more *bioavailable* calcium than a gallon of milk! While greens are vegetables, they are so important in our daily diets that I have given them an entire section all their own.

While the baby greens are best served raw, most members of the cruciferous family, namely cabbages, Brussels sprouts, broccoli, bok choy, kale and chard benefit from a light steaming or hold up to longer cooking making them perfect for soups and casseroles. Many greens are a staple of Southern cooking like spicy turnip greens, collard greens, mature beet greens and spinach, because they are cool weather crops that can be grown even in the winter months. Each and every variety of green can be considered a powerful nutritional addition to any meal; so choosing the top 3 was difficult (so I cheated a little). Here are the 3 OMG! Nutritional All-Stars of greens – endive, mixed baby field greens and kale.

There are two distinctly different forms of endive curly and Belgian. While you may be accustomed to some curly endive in your mixed greens, Belgian endive is likely one of those salad greens you pass over, simply because it's so rarely used in recipes you may not know how to serve them. However, recent research has connected these tender yet crunchy, slightly bitter, delicious little boat shaped leaves to some very important health benefits.

While they can be eaten raw, braised, or added to soups, when eaten raw they act as powerful digestive agents due to the high levels of inulin and prebiotics they contain. However in all forms their slight bitterness stimulates the liver to produce more bile resulting in better digestion as well as liver detoxification. Combined with their relatively high fiber content means that the wastes are effectively carried out of the body. While these alone are a good reason to eat endive, it's also been shown to reduce LDL cholesterol and regulate blood sugar. Nutritionally speaking, it's high in B vitamins including folate, beta-carotene, manganese, copper, iron, potassium, magnesium and phosphorus, which are cofactors for producing a very powerful antioxidant, superoxide dismutase (SOD) as well as an excellent source for balancing electrolytes.

Raw greens like mixed baby field greens provide a wide array of greens at the peak of their flavor and nutritional content. These mixes combine very young spinach, arugula, dandelion and beet greens with a mix of baby Romaine, tat soi, butter, red leaf and curly endive lettuces, to provide spectacular taste, texture and nutrition. In fact one salad made from raw baby mixed greens can provide up to 80% of your beta-carotene and 74% of your folate needs for the entire day! All of that and they are excellent sources of fiber, calcium, magnesium, iron and Vitamins C and E, making them a powerful source of antioxidants and anti-inflammatory agents.

This unique nutritional profile has led researchers to the conclusion that women who eat at least one serving of raw baby greens 5 times a week significantly lower their risk of breast cancer. When combined with some of the veggies, oil and vinegar profiled below you will understand why I cheated a bit and do consider these tasty and powerful greens a part of that special list of OMG! All-Stars!

In the world of veggies, greens are the kings, but **kale** is the supreme ruler of the kingdom! There is so much nutritional and health benefit data available on this one green that I could write an entire book and cookbook showcasing it! Due to space constraints, I'm going to focus on only a few of its benefits starting with its nutritional profile. A single cup of steamed kale provides 1325% of Vitamin K, 193% of Vitamin A, 90% of Vitamin C, 30% of manganese and more than 10% of calcium, copper, tryptophan, Vitamins B1 B2 B3 B6 and folate, potassium, iron, magnesium, Vitamin E, Omega 3 fatty acids, phosphorus and protein! While all of that is staggering, read on to see just what that does in your body . . .

1 cup of steamed kale 3-4 times a week has been shown to significantly reduce the risk factors for bladder, breast, colon, ovarian and prostate cancers. That is impressive, but it's only scratching the surface. Kale contains compounds known as isothiocyanates and approximately 45 flavonoids that work in combination to produce anti-inflammatories and antioxidants that are more powerful than any laboratory can currently produce. And if that's not enough to convince you to add some kale to your diet, those same ITC's actually support detoxification at a genetic level. While there are some other powerful foods in the OMG! All-Star list, kale is unarguably at the top of the food list!

Veggies

Eating a healthy diet is all about using food as medicine and there is no food group that contains more medicinal qualities than veggies! From crunchy celery and fennel to creamy artichokes and potatoes, from fiery peppers, turnips and radishes to cool and sweet tomatoes, squashes and cucumbers, from dark green broccoli rabe to creamy white cauliflower, from bright red, yellow and orange peppers to stunning purple eggplant and beets, veggies provide the greatest variety you can hope for in any meal!

While all this variety in color and texture adds a great deal of interest to our plates, each of these veggies contain key components that round out the nutritional profile of each and every meal. In fact the nutritional value some veggies are actually enhanced or increased when served in combination (like kale and tomatoes or tomatoes and olives - I know, these are technically fruits). But there are 3 standouts in this category that make them worthy of the OMG! All-Stars of Veggies, **garlic, avocados and sweet potatoes.**

Garlic has long been considered a great way to ward off vampires but you may not know it is equally good at protecting our blood vessels and red blood cells from the ravages of oxidation and inflammation. In fact it has more than 16 sulfur containing constituents that provide this protection! Additionally, it lowers triglyceride levels, protects LDL cholesterol from oxidation (and that prevents plaque buildup), regulates clotting factors, thins the blood, regulates blood pressure and blood sugars, is a powerful anti-microbial, lowers the risk of all known cancers and enhances the utilization of iron. And if that were not reason enough to add some flavor to your next dish, garlic is a good source of manganese and selenium which are co-factors for the most powerful antioxidant our own bodies produce – glutathione

At first glance no one would ever guess that **avocados** held such a treasure trove of health benefits in the luscious, creamy flesh below that rather unappealing leathery exterior! Long avoided by many for their high fat content, this misunderstood fruit is now considered a champion in the fight against cardiovascular disease (including cholesterol issues), cancer, arthritis and nervous system disorders.

It seems that the combination of oleic acids, fiber, polyhydroxylated fatty alcohols (PFA's are generally only found in sea vegetables) and spectacular array of carotenoids are so unique that scientists are puzzled by their findings.

Plus the avocados mix of fat soluble carotenoids, which mostly lie in the dark green outer coating that lies just below the leathery skin, when combined with the unique fats in the flesh, deliver anti-inflammatory and antioxidant benefits that are relatively unparalleled! In fact avocados have the unique ability to protect healthy cells from oxidation while increasing the oxidation levels in cancer cells which leads them to a quick self-destruction (apoptosis). That makes avocados one of the OMG! All-Stars of this category!

Sweet potatoes, often mislabeled as yams, are absolutely one of the most important stars of the veggie show! In addition to their astonishing levels of Vitamin A (in the form of beta-carotene), sweet potatoes also contain anthocyanin pigments which produce powerful antioxidants and anti-inflammatories. Additionally, sweet potatoes contain an interesting storage protein, sporamins, which allows them to "self-heal" from damage during harvesting and storage. This same antioxidant characteristic is utilized by our cells.

Sweet potatoes are considered by many to be a functional food. Functional foods are classified this way because while their nutritional profile may be impressive their health benefits surpass their individual components. For example a single protein in sweet potatoes improves blood sugar regulation by increasing the production of a hormone that modifies insulin metabolism. They also contain powerful antibacterial and antifungal agents and the purple skinned varieties contain 3 times more antioxidants than blueberries.

Eating ½ cup of baked, steamed or roasted sweet potatoes 3-4 times a week has been demonstrated to regulate blood clotting factors, protect the myelin sheath around nerve fibers, improve blood sugar regulation, to increase eye health and this is just the beginning! So whether you try sweet potato hash, pumpkin waffles or muffins (actually made with sweet potatoes), a salad with roasted sweet potatoes or baked with a little compound butter, you will see why I added these delicious root veggies to my OMG! All-Star list!

Fruit

Like vegetables, there is such a beautiful array of fruits available to us with each season! From stone fruits like peaches, plums, apricots and cherries to melons like cantaloupe, honeydew and watermelon, from juicy pears to apples in every size, shape and color, from exotic papaya, pineapple and coconuts to jewel toned berries, in every season fruit is bountiful, beautiful and packed with vitamins, minerals and fiber!

In addition to all of that fruit is portable, versatile and can be frozen and dried without losing its nutritional value. Incorporating fruit into

smoothies, appetizers, main dishes, salads and desserts is a delicious way to instantly boost the nutritional content of any meal!

Of all the vast array of fruit these 3 OMG! Nutritional Allstars offer some of the best healing properties, **watermelon, coconut and berries!**

The quintessential fruit of summer, **watermelon** has the distinction of providing the greatest nutritional content per calorie than any other fruit! Grown in hot climates, its unique vitamin and mineral components have been proven to be the best way to balance your electrolytes after a hot day in the sun. It seems nature knows best . . .

In addition to its high Vitamin A, B and C contents, watermelon is also high in potassium, magnesium and lycopene. These constituents may shed some light on its high antioxidant and anti-inflammatory properties. In fact watermelon has been shown to help macular degeneration, prevent erectile dysfunction, improve insulin sensitivity, prevent prostate and colon cancers, asthma, arthritis, diabetes and the little black seeds also lower blood pressure!

Coconut, like watermelon is something of a wonder cure! From the electrolyte rich water of young coconuts (which is sometimes used in place of blood plasma), to the dried flesh and oils from the more mature fruits; every part of the coconut has invaluable health benefits. Like the avocado, it's benefits reach far beyond its nutritional profile, elevating it to the category of a functional food.

As an antimicrobial agent it has been shown to effectively destroy a wide variety of viruses, bacteria, fungi and parasites including this rather impressive list: herpes, measles, hepatitis C, AIDS, UTI's, cavities, periodontal disease, ringworm, athlete's foot, tapeworms, lice and giardia just to name a few.

Another long and impressive list of maladies the coconut has been shown to help with include the following: the ratio of HDL to LDL cholesterol, improves thyroid function, protects fatty acids from oxidation, dissolves kidney stones, increases metabolic rate, acts as a powerful anti-inflammatory and antioxidant. Making it an unarguable addition to my OMG! All-Star list!

Common **berries**, including raspberries, cranberries, blackberries, Marion berries, lingon berries, strawberries, blueberries and huckleberries are among the most potent antioxidant carriers in the world! These delicious little fruits may be a bit delicate, but they certainly pack a nutritional punch that is undeniably effective!

Each berry has a unique nutritional profile, which renders it more helpful to the brain, the urinary tract, the lungs, etc, but what all berries have in common is their ability to combat the free radicals that are the culprits behind aging, disease and death.   This is primarily due to their high levels of Vitamin C, manganese and fiber. So it's easy to see why eating a cup of delicious berries a day can keep the plastic surgeon at bay!

Animal Based Proteins

When choosing animal based proteins there are a few things to keep in mind . . .look for land based animal based proteins that are free range and organic. These animals have been fed food free from harmful pesticides and herbicides, and they have not been given antibiotics. When possible find a local farm that offers these products.

Purchase only cold water, line caught fish from Alaska, British Columbia and Washington State. These fish have been shown to demonstrate very low levels of pesticides, growth hormones and toxins associated with warm water seafood. Soon there will be a "certified organic" designation for fish and shellfish as well, be on the lookout for it!

Some people who demonstrate allergies to eggs from caged hens do not demonstrate the same allergy to fresh, organic, free-range eggs. At this time I can only conjecture that is has to do with antibiotics, growth hormones and the poor quality feed given to the caged hens which results in high levels of stress hormones.

Having lived in the northwest, where both fresh and frozen Alaskan, line caught **salmon** and **halibut** are staples in the diet, I have come to truly appreciate the accolades due these cold-water fish. Line caught, Alaskan varieties are among the best sources of Omega 3's in the world. In fact eating only small amounts of salmon weekly make significant changes in the Omega 3 content of the membranes of red blood cells. This change coupled with their nutritional profiles account for the remarkable changes it can make in cellular health.

Additionally, salmon contains over 100% of the RDA of tryptophan, Vitamin D and significantly more than 50% of B12, B6, selenium, phosphorus and protein. Halibut has even higher levels of selenium and protein but slightly lower levels of B vitamins. These statistics demonstrate why a diet that includes these two OMG! All-Stars will do your body good!

While I do not have the answer to the age-old debate of which came first the chicken or the egg, I do believe that if the two were involved in a nutritional competition, the egg would be the clear winner! Only recently has the incredible, edible egg regained its reputation as a nearly perfect food. However there is a caveat to their status . . . only fresh, organic, free-range eggs make it on my list of **OMG! Nutritional All-Stars.**

Eggs are an excellent source of choline, the newest member of the family of B vitamins. Choline plays several key roles in the body including enhancing proper brain function, increasing proper communication between nerve and muscle fibers, decreasing inflammation and most importantly, keeping cell membranes supple and healthy.

Additionally, eggs are an excellent source of high quality, low cost and low calorie protein plus tryptophan, selenium, iodine, lutein, Vitamins B 2, B 5, B 12 and D. This profile has been linked to lowering risk factors for macular degeneration, cataracts, blood clots and strokes as well as breast cancer!

Hippocrates first mentioned adverse reactions to cow's milk in about 370 B.C. While more than 60% of the world's population is allergic to cow's milk, less than 20% are allergic to milk from goats and sheep and an even smaller percentage to milk from water buffalo. This is due in large part to the type of caseines and short chain sugars contained in these milks.

While water buffalo, goat and sheep's milk have been used for centuries to produce flavorful yogurts and cheeses, in the last decade the cheese industry has changed and now there are endless varieties of delicious cheeses produced from these sources. While I do not recommend consuming large quantities of any dairy products, if you can tolerate these items, they are a good source of protein and do offer a wide range of minerals, amino acids and probiotics.

Legumes

In the plant world few foods offer the same level of health benefits found in **legumes**. All types of beans and all colors of beans, from black beans to green lentils to white navy beans, offer the highest levels of both soluble and insoluble fibers of any food.

One study alone has shown that eating a high fiber diet has many benefits including, a 15% decrease in cardiovascular disease, a 12% decrease in diabetes and a 10% decrease in cancer! If that was not motivation enough to eat some beans, here are some more rather impressive reasons to include a wide variety of beans in your diet. . .

All beans are excellent sources of protein, folate and minerals, particularly manganese. Manganese is a key mineral in the production of superoxide dismutase (SOD), an extremely powerful antioxidant that neutralizes free radicals in the mitochondria, the part of the cell where the energy to fuel the cell is produced. Even relatively small amounts of oxidative damage to the mitochondria will cause a cell to either mutate or die, resulting in lower overall energy as well as lifestyle diseases like heart disease, diabetes, fibromyalgia, chronic fatigue and cancer.

While each variety will have a slightly different ratio of protein to fiber, they all fall within the range of 15-22 grams of each! This ratio is completely unique in high protein foods. When coupled with the complex carbohydrates and the low levels of fats found in legumes, it leads many to believe that they are a nearly perfect food. Their unique constituents account for their outstanding ability to regulate blood sugars, protect the cells lining the colon from carcinogens, provide a long lasting supply of energy, suppress the appetite, increase oxygenation in the tissues and regulate blood clotting factors, just to name a few!

Some studies indicate that the darker colored beans like black, adzuki, red kidney, French lentils and even lima beans have a few extra benefits, but I believe that **all beans deserve the designation of being OMG! Nutritional All-Stars!**

Miscellaneous

Nutritional yeast, seaweed, vinegar, chocolate and a few oils are all OMG! All-Stars but don't fit well into any of the categories above. So to save time and space I'm going to include only their most impressive health benefits.

Nutritional yeast, unlike yeast used in baking, is deactivated yeast, making it free of candida albicans. Available in flakes or powder, I use the flakes because I prefer their taste and texture. Just two tablespoons of fortified nutritional yeast

flakes, contains a significant amount of fiber, protein, beta-1,3 glucan (a fiber that boost the immune system and lowers cholesterol), iron, potassium, SOD building selenium and most impressively, very high amounts of an array of Vitamin B's, including 150% of the RDA of Vitamin B12 and 750% of riboflavin, making it an absolute OMG! All-Star for all vegetarians and everyone following a GF diet!

There are a host of **sea vegetables** that offer astounding health benefits, but the most important of these is iodine. Iodine is a crucial mineral missing from most diets. Found primarily in seaweed and cold-water seafood (not fresh water or farm raised fish), this all important trace mineral is essential for proper thyroid function. Iodine assists proper thyroid function by regulating the production of hormones that are directly associated with our metabolic rate. The other important function of iodine lies in its regulation of programmed cell death (apoptosis), which is crucial to healthy organ function as well as cancer prevention. The best seaweed options are dulce, hijiki, wakami, nori and kelp.

Vinegar, especially apple cider, coconut and wine vinegars are acids that help our bodies with digestion in a few very interesting ways! Vinegar encourages the proper production of hydrochloric acid which is necessary for the digestion of protien. Plus it stops acid refux in this way – there is a sphincter at the base of the esophagus responsible for keeping the contents of our stomach in our stomach. However, it will not close until it senses an adequate amount of acid in the stomach. Adding vinegar to a meal will increase the amount of acid in the stomach ensuring the proper closure of the sphincter which stops the reverse flow of acids up the esophagus while increasing digestion! That's a winning combination!

My daughter Angela has always believed that **chocolate** should be its own food group, and she may be on to something! Raw cacao is now considered the most powerful antioxidant in the world due to its content of flavanols (a flavanoid only found in chocolate)! And it alone maintains all of its antioxidant power even when exposed to air during processing and storage! Raw cacao and dark chocolate's antioxidant benefits have been linked to stroke prevention, protection of LDL against oxidation, regulating blood pressure, cancer prevention and tooth decay (as long as it doesn't contain too much sugar)! Cacao contains more magnesium than any other plant as well as serotonin for mood stabilization, which is why some women crave it during their monthly cycles.

Oils from many plant sources are amazing sources of the heart healthy forms of Vitamin E. While each oil contains its unique profile of fats, fatty acids, vitamins and minerals, the oils that top this category for me are coconut, extra virgin olive oil, pecan oil, walnut oil, almond oil, flax oil and pumpkin seed oil. These oils have been proven to protect you from your brain to your prostate and from your skin to your liver! Add at least one of these OMG! All-Star oils to your diet daily!

I hope you find this information both inspirational and helpful. For more in-depth nutritional profiles, health benefits and clinical data please visit my website at www.SimpleHealthNetwork.com or my blog at www.OMGAllergyFree.com.

Dairy Alternatives

Hippocrates was the first physician on record to mention cow's milk allergies in 370 B.C. Today allergy or intolerance to cow's milk affects slightly more than 1 out of every 2 people worldwide . . . in other words more than half of the population!

Yet many of our favorite comfort foods contain large amounts of milk, cream and cheese! From pizza, pasta and sauces to pudding, ice cream and even cream cheese icing, cow's milk is the common ingredient in them all.

But there's no reason to despair . . . in this section you will find delicious alternatives to these dairy products. From delicious milks and diary substitutes made from nuts to lucious whipped topping made from coconut milk and cheeses made from nuts or goat and sheep's milk yogurt, you're sure to find substitutes for all of the dairy products you've been missing!

Not only are these alternatives absolutely delicious, they are far more nutritious as well! Nuts, seeds, coconut and nutritional yeast are all nutritional powerhouses packed with vitamins, minerals, probiotics and healthy fats that are easy to digest.

So dust off your food processor, buy some cheesecloth and become your own gourmet cheese maker!   Your favorite cheesy comfort foods are back!

Soy Whipped Topping

This was an accidental discovery that turned out to be a great substitute for sweetened whipped cream or meringue because it's very much like a combination of the two. Soft and fluffy with a glossy sheen it will impress you with its texture and flavor!
Yield – 1 1/4 cups

1 cup unsweetened organic Silk soymilk
1 tablespoon agave nectar
1 1/2 teaspoons vanilla extract
1/4 xanthan or guar gum

Bring soymilk to a slow simmer and reduce by half. Cool to room temperature then add agave and vanilla. Whip with an electric mixer on low while incorporating the xanthan gum, increase to high and whip until the volume is at least doubled and forms lovely soft peaks.

Your whipped topping will keep up to a week, simply stir it gently before using as a whipped cream substitute. As a meringue it will set with very shiny peaks in just a few minutes. The peaks will flatten out a bit over time, so it is best to top your pie or other dessert not more than an hour before serving.

Sweet Almond Crème

This is a simplified version that produces a thick and creamy non-dairy topping to use on your favorite pies, cobblers and crisps. It makes soft, creamy puddles rather than stiff peaks. Use within 48 hours.
Yield – 1 cup

1/2 cup Very Vanilla Almond Milk
3/4 cup soaked blanched Almonds
3 Pitted Dates
1/2 inch piece Vanilla Bean
1/4 tsp Xanthan or Guar Gum

Place almonds, almond milk, dates and vanilla bean in VitaMix and blend until completely liquefied. Add xanthan gum and blend. Place in a glass bowl with a lid and refrigerate 2 hours or overnight.

Coconut Crème

Here is a great substitute for whipped cream, especially on chocolate desserts – warm GF brownies are my favorite! While it retains it's form on cool desserts, like all whipped topping it melts rather quickly on a warm dessert, so use this topping at the last moment. I keep this in my refrigerator regularly because it is such a versatile topping. Refrigerate up to 2 weeks. Yield – 1 3/4 cups

14 oz can Thai Kitchen organic coconut milk
1/8 teaspoon xanthan or guar gum

Refrigerate can for at least 1 hour. Open and spoon the thick creamy coconut milk into a medium sized mixing bowl and whip until almost doubled in volume. Reserve remaining thin coconut milk for use in another recipe.

If the whipped coconut milk looks too thick add up to 1/4 cup of the thin coconut milk, one tablespoon at a time. Store in a glass bowl or jar with a tight fitting lid. Refrigerate up to 10 days.

This whipped creme can become a bit stiff in the refrigerator, if this happens simply whisk or beat until the soft peaks return.

Unsweetened Almond Milk

This is a great "go to" milk that has all the nutritional benefits of almonds and is much less expensive to make than to purchase. This recipe produces a milk more similar to whole milk than is commercially available.
Yield - 7 cups

2 cups raw organic almonds
4 cups pH 11.5 ionized water*
6 cups pH 9.5 ionized water*

Soak almonds in 4 cups pH 11.5 water 4 hours or overnight in a glass jar with a lid. Drain off water, place nuts and 9.5 Ionized Water into a VitaMix or powerful blender. Blend on the highest speed for approximately 2-3 minutes until nuts are liquefied. Strain through a bag. Discard the solids and store the almond milk in the refrigerator for up to 3 days.

*Filtered water can be substituted. Ionized water at this pH breaks down the fats in the nuts better which results in a more complete breakdown of the almonds. This produces a smoother milk with less solids to strain out.

Very Vanilla Almond Milk

Slightly sweetened from the addition of dates combined with 2 types of real vanilla makes this a great addition to your smoothie, cereal, tea or ice cold with some freshly baked cookies, or use it in recipes like sweet biscuits.
Yield - 7 cups

7 cups Unsweetened Almond Milk
3 pitted dates or 1/4 tsp Stevia
1 tsp high quality real Vanilla Extract
1/2 inch piece of Vanilla Bean*

*No need to split and scrape the seeds from the pod simply toss in the VitaMix and all fibrous portions will be strained out in in the bag. The pod is also very flavorful so a smaller piece produces a bold flavor. If you don't have the dried vanilla bean you can adjust the amount of vanilla extract to suite your own taste.

Pine Nut, Cashew and Macadamia Ricotta

This cheeze is very rich, very thick and mildly flavorful just like its cow's milk cousin, making it a truly great substitute! The texture is fantastic and because of the high fat content in both the pine nuts and the macadamias it mimics whole milk ricotta. These nuts are packed with nutrition; in fact cashews have been demonstrated to prevent colon cancer, healthy fats and fiber. The miso is loaded with enzymes and each ingredient offers a wide array of minerals, making this an ultra-healthy, and very yummy, substitute for cow's milk. It can be used in such a wide variety of ways, from Roasted Vegetable Lasagne to Lemon Ricotta Ice Crème with Tart Cherries and Pistachios.
Yield – 3 1/2 cups

1 1/4 cups pine nuts
1/2 cup macadamia nuts
1/2 cup raw cashews
6 cups pH 9.5 ionized water
3 tablespoons lemon juice
2 tablespoons white miso
1 teaspoon tahini
2 tablespoons nutritional yeast
1/4 teaspoon Celtic sea salt

Soak nuts in pH 9.5 ionized water at least 6 hours, overnight is best, rinse and drain well. Place in food processor or Vita-Mix blender and process until very smooth. If necessary, add water 1 tablespoon at a time to facilitate processing. Taste and adjust seasonings if necessary.

Store in a glass bowl or jar with a tight fitting lid up to 10 days.

NOTE: If using solely in savory dishes I add 2 teaspoons roasted garlic and 1/2 teaspoon white pepper as a flavor boost. If using solely in sweet dishes I add 1 teaspoon fine lemon zest.

Nutrition Note: Nuts are among the most nutritious plant based protein sources. Since they are a great source for heart healthy oils, a wide variety of minerals, vitamins as well as antioxidants, eating 1 ounce of nuts per day has been linked to prevention of gall stones, heart disease, bone and muscle loss as well as a reduction in triglycerides and diabetic neuropathy.

Blue Cheeze

Stir the following into the Ricotta recipe above and you will have a substitute to regular blue cheese.
Yield - 4 cups

Soak, drain and process 1/2 cup pistachios with 1 tablespoon lemon juice, 1 tablespoon yellow miso, 1 teaspoon tahini, 3 cloves minced garlic, 1 tablespoon nutritional yeast and 2 teaspoons roasted pistachio oil

Swirl into ricotta, place into a cheesecloth lined mesh strainer and drain 6 hours or until it is a thick, creamy cheese.

Olives and Feta

This is a wonderful blend of flavorful olives and crumbled feta in olive oil. Over time it becomes something like a creamy, cheezy tapinade. I've seen it in Middle Eastern gourmet shops, and now you can make it yourself! Serve it with Spelt or GF No Knead Ciabatta or GF Goat Cheese Crackers. It's positively addictive!
Yield - 2 cups

3/4 cup Baked and crumbled Almond Feta Cheeze or sheep's milk feta
3/4 cup chopped mixed olives - I prefer Greek blend
1/3 cup Herbed Olive Oil
3 sundried tomatoes, diced
1 teaspoon Bruschetta Spice Blend
1 rounded teaspoon capers

Place in a glass jar add enough brine from feta so the entire mixture is covered in olive oil, cover and refrigerate.

Marinated Feta

Whether made from sheep's milk or nut milk, feta is delicious when marinated. It can add another layer of flavor to a quick salad or a main dish, to sanwiches or savory muffins. It's a great staple to keep in your refrigerator. Be certain that the feta is covered with oil to ensure it remains preserved. It will keep for several weeks.
Yield – 1 cup

1 cup sheep's milk feta cubed or Feta Cheeze, cut into cubes or crumbled
2 tablespoons Middle Eastern Spice or Bruschetta Spice Blend
1/4 teaspoon red pepper flakes
Herbed Olive Oil and brine to cover

In a small bowl whisk spice blend, red pepper flakes and 1/4 cup olive oil together, then add feta and carefully stir to coat. Carefully spoon into a jar and add enough of the brine or whey from the feta to cover completely.

To use, simply spoon out the desired amount, taking care that remaining feta is covered by the oil.

Refrigerated and completely covered it will keep at least 2 weeks.

Marinated Feta can be used within an hour, but the longer it marinates the more flavorful it becomes, so if possible marinate overnight.

Once you have used all of the feta, the oil can be used in a marinade or vinaigrette to add an extra layer of flavor to your dish.

Yogurt Style Cheeses

This is a great, inexpensive way to make soft cheese, crème fraiche, sour cream and cream cheese substitutes from your favorite plain, unsweetened yogurt, and one of the easiest things you've ever done. Be sure to try some of the variations.

Determine how much soft cheese, crème fraiche or sour cream you want at the end of the process using the following guide lines: 1 1/4 cups yogurt yields approximately 1/3 cup soft cheese, 1/2 cup cream cheese, 2/3 cup ricotta and mascarpone, 3/4 cup sour créme and 1 cup créme fraiche.

To make any of these substitutes you will need a large colander, that fits over a bowl, lined with several layers of cheesecloth, paper coffee filters or a fine mesh strainer bag and a little patience. I recommend that you purchase at least 1 large container of goat or sheep's milk yogurt, divide and start several of these recipes.

Crème Fraîche Substitute

Traditionally a soft blend of fresh cream and sour cream, so less tang, a tiny bit of sweetness and very soft puddles of creamy goodness. It's used in both sweet and savory dishes, so it has a great deal of versatility. This version is a very close replica.
Yield – 3/4 cup

1 1/4 cups plain goat or sheep's milk yogurt
1/2 teaspoon agave nectar
1 pinch xanthan or guar gum
1 pinch Celtic sea salt

Mix thoroughly and place in a wire mesh strainer that has been lined with a paper coffee filter or a triple layer of cheese cloth, placed over a bowl. Drain 2-3 hours or until desired consistency. Spoon into a glass container with a tight fitting lid and refrigerate up to 2 weeks.

Maple Crème Fraîche

This is a great topping for my Pumpkin Pie Smoothie, Pumpkin Custard, Crepes with Sautéed Apples or Pumpkin & Toasted Walnut Waffles or even a cup of chai tea.
Yield – 3/4 cup

1 8 ounce container Old Chatham's maple sheep's milk yogurt
OR 8 ounces of your favorite plain yogurt mixed with 1 tablespoon grade "B" maple syrup
1/2 teaspoon Fall Spice Blend
1/4 teaspoon good quality vanilla extract

Mix thoroughly and place in a wire mesh strainer that has been lined with a paper coffee filter or a triple layer of cheese cloth, placed over a bowl. Drain for 2-3 hours. Spoon into a glass container with a tightly fitting lid and refrigerate up to 2 weeks. Before serving, blend with an immersion blender or beat with mixer to incorporate a little "airiness" into your topping.

 Coconut or Almond Creme Fraîche and Sour Crème

This style is made from So Delicious or Amonde yogurt which both offer a fairly bland taste, resulting in the opportunity to impart the flavors you choose. I think it works great in many Thai soups, as well as my Sweet Potato and Brazil Nut Creme Soup or over pound cake with a few fresh berries. The addition of nutritional yeast provides a slight cheesy flavor and the vinegar provides a touch of the tang we associate with sour cream and creme fraiche.
Yield - 1 cup

1 8 ounce container So Delicious plain yogurt
1 teaspoon nutritional yeast
1/8 teaspoon Celtic sea salt
1 pinch xanthan or guar gum
1/4 teaspoon coconut vinegar

Blend well and set aside for at least 30 minutes to allow flavors to meld. Beat with electric mixer on high speed for 2-3 minutes.

Riocotta Cheese Substitute

Ricotta should be light, have a somewhat neutral taste and blend well with lots of other flavors, from sweet to savory, melt creamy, becoming almost sauce like. It is one of those staples of Italian cuisine that I missed so very much! When I visited Central Market in Dallas I found that the Dallas Mozzarella Company produces a goat's milk ricotta that is wonderful. However it's not available nationwide, so I decided to try making a substitute and it is convincingly good, and I actually like the texture a bit better. Plus it contains all of those great beneficial lactobacillus and acidophilus strains that aide in digestion and intestinal health and it's packed with trace minerals and Vitamin B's, it's lower in fat . . . what else could you want!
Yield 2 1/2 cups

4 cups goat or sheep's milk yogurt
1 1/2 teaspoons nutritional yeast
1/2 rounded teaspoon xanthan or guar gum
1/4 rounded teaspoon Celtic sea salt
1 teaspoon lemon juice

If you have a specific purpose for your ricotta keep this in mind, goat's milk yogurt makes a slightly better ricotta for savory dishes and sheep's milk yogurt works slightly better for sweet dishes.

Traditionally ricotta is cooked and slightly grainy in texture. The addition of extra xanthan gum will produce that grainy texture, but I prefer it to be a bit smooth. Feel free to try up to 3/4 teaspoon if you like.

Mix all ingredients well and place in a mesh strainer that has been lined with a double layer of coffee filters or a triple layer of cheesecloth that has been placed over a bowl. Cover lightly and drain 12-18 hours, depending upon both temperature and humidity, until it is thick, but spreadable.

Use in any recipe calling for ricotta. Store, refrigerated, in a glass jar with a tight fitting lid, up to 2 weeks.

Mascarpone Cheese Substitute

Mascarpone cheese is a double or triple cream, fresh cow's milk cheese that is used frequently in Italian style desserts, appetizers and sauces. In Italian the word means "better than good" and it is. Those of us who are allergic to cow's milk have had to forego great desserts like tiramisu and cannoli as well as luscious tarts and decadent appetizers until now!

I have discovered a great substitute for traditional mascarpone that has a thick, luxurious texture, it's slightly sweet and tangy with the same overtones of lavender and lemon that makes traditional mascarpone so luscious.
Yield – 2 1/2 cups

4 cups goat or sheep's milk yogurt
3 inch strip lemon zest
1 inch strip of orange zest
1 tablespoon lemon juice
1 sprig of fresh lavender or 8 lavender flowers
4 teaspoons clover honey
1/4 teaspoon nutritional yeast
 1/4 teaspoon guar or xanthan gum

To make your mascarpone substitute you will need the best quality sheep or goat's milk yogurt. I prefer a mix of Bellweth-er Farms Sheep's milk yogurt and Redwood Hills Farm's goat yogurt, although you can use any yogurt you like.
Combine all ingredients. Line a strainer or colander with a double layer of paper coffee liners or quadrupled cheesecloth and place over a bowl. Fill with yogurt mixture and allow to drain 12 - 18 hours or until desired consistency is achieved. It should be very thick, creamy yet still spreadable.   Remove the lavender sprigs and citrus zest. Place in bowl, cover and refrigerate until ready to use. Refrigerated it will keep approximately 2 weeks.

Crème Cheese Substitute

This crème is thick and spreadable and better than any light cream cheese. It is nutrient dense and guilt free!
Yield – 1/2 cup

1 1/4 cups plain yogurt
1/4 teaspoon agave nectar
3/4 teaspoon nutritional yeast
1/4 teaspoon xanthan or guar gum
1/4 teaspoon Celtic sea salt

Mix thoroughly and place in a wire mesh strainer that has been lined with a double layer of paper coffee filters or a triple layer of cheese cloth, placed over a bowl. Drain 12-16 hours. Spoon into a glass container with a tightly fitting lid and refrigerate up to 2 weeks. Stir before serving.

Yogurt Cheese

Yogurt cheese is very common in East Indian cuisine. It is so close to goat cheese in texture that it's difficult to tell them apart. However, yogurt cheese is much lower in fat and with the addition of nutritional yeast to the recipe, it is both nutrient dense and filled with super healthy probiotics.
Yield – 1/3 cup

1 1/4 cups plain yogurt
1 teaspoon nutritional yeast
1/4 teaspoon xanthan or guar gum
1/4 teaspoon Celtic sea salt

Mix thoroughly and place in a wire mesh strainer that has been lined with a double layer of paper coffee filters or a triple layer of cheese cloth, placed over a bowl. Drain 18 - 24 hours or until very thick and barely spreadable. Roll into a log or spoon into a glass container with a tightly fitting lid and refrigerate up to 2 weeks.

Fruit and Nut Cheeses

This is so delicious on Goat Cheese Crackers or pear slices and it is as easy as stirring in your favorite fruit sweetened jam, some dired friut and rolling in your favorite chopped nuts.   I like black cherry jam, chopped dried cherries and chopped almonds; apricot jam, chopped apricots and almonds; orange marmalade, Candied Citrus Peel and pistachios. There are so many others . . . just let yourself be creative.

Yield - 5 inch log

1/3 cup Yogurt Cheese
2 tablespoons fruit sweetened jam
2 tablespoons chopped nuts

Stir jam into cheese in a swirl pattern. Shape into a log and roll in nuts. Wrap in parchment or waxed paper, then plastic wrap and store in refrigerator.

Sharp and Tangy Blue Cheese

This is an amazing combination. I found a fresh goat cheese and goat blue cheese combo at my local Whole Foods market and decided to give this a try. It is so simple, lovely and balanced. The salty and sharp sheep's milk Roquerfort and the creamy smooth and tangy cheese were made for one another! In thls verslon I used sheep's milk yogurt to make the cheese and it is so perfect! I used some of this cheese to make the Goat Cheese Crackers with Blue Cheese and Thyme in the photo. They are amazing!
Yield - 3 inch ball

1/3 cup Yogurt Cheese
1 1/2 tablespoons Roquerfort, crumbled

Mix together, taking care to leave some of the small crumbles intact. Shape into a ball. Store in a flat bottomed bowl with a tight fitting lid up to 2 weeks.

Sugar and Spice and . . .

This section includes recipes to create your own high end spice blends, superfine sugars, salt blends, flavored nuts, quick pickles, roasted veggies and GF flour blends. No need to visit a gormet kitchen shop, they are simple to make and save you lots of time, tons of money and help you cook like a professional chef . . . so fill your pantry with these essentials!

Sugar Blends - Superfine sugars are the friends of chefs and bartenders the world round. They are ground into a very fine texture that melts quickly and easily, improving texture in many baked goods. They are simple to make, and subtly enhance flavor.

Salt Blends - A salt blend is one of the easiest ways to add layers of flavor to a simple preparation of veggies, grilled foods, plain rice or quinoa while keeping your salt intake in check. Once you've made the blend simply pop it into a salt grinder and with every turn you add a touch of extra flavor.

Spice Blends - Making your own spice blends can really speed up prep time when cooking. There are a few I use so often that I find it easier to make my own than to purchase a small bottle, and it is much more cost effective. Most natural foods markets have a bulk herb and spice section where the prices are considerably lower.

GF Flour Blends - There are so many blends available, but in my experience most of them fall short of producing a really good end product. I have 2 that I use when nuts are not an option in a recipe. They have a bit more nutritional value than most that are available and I think you will find they produce consistent results.

Superfine Vanilla Sugar

This sugar is delicate with floral overtones. It is a wonderful addition to shortcakes, scones and chocolate or coconut desserts.
Yield – 2 cups

2 cups evaporated cane juice or palm sugar
1-2 inch piece of spent vanilla bean

Place both in food processor and pulse until vanilla bean has been chopped into a few smaller pieces. Process until vanilla bean is completely incorporated and the sugar has been broken into very small crystals.

Spread out on a piece of parchment paper to and dry completely. Transfer to a small glass jar with a tight fitting lid. This will keep indefinitely.

Superfine Citrus Sugar

This adds a lot of subtle flavor to cookies, cocktails, desserts and even a cup of tea. The flavor lasts so long that it's definitely worth making.

2 cups evaporated cane juice or palm sugar
2 tablespoons lemon, orange or lime zest

Place both in food processor and pulse until zest is completely incorporated and the sugar has been broken into very small crystals.

Spread out on a piece of parchment paper to dry completely. Since citrus fruits contain a great deal of oil in their rinds, this will make your sugar a bit sticky so it will take a bit more time to dry out. Once dry, return to the food processor for another minute of processing. Transfer to a small glass jar with a tight fitting lid. Keeps up to 1 year.

Superfine Chai Spice Sugar

I love the warm spices that are found in chai tea. This flavorful sugar is a terrific addition to pumpkin desserts, Soy Whipped Crème, Chai Latte Ice Crème and so much more!
Yield - 2 cups

2 cups palm, maple or date sugar
1 tablespoon Chai Spice Blend

Unlike delicate citrus oils, chai spices can hold up to the bold flavors of date or maple sugar, so don't be afraid to experiment! Place sugar and spices in food processor and pulse until zest is completely incorporated and the sugar has been broken into very small crystals. Transfer to a small glass jar with a tight fitting lid. This will keep up to 6 months, then the spices will begin to

Mediterranean Blend Sea Salt

This blend is a wonderful and flavorful addition to soups, roasted veggies and fish.
Yield – 2/3 cup

1/2 cup coarse sea salt
1 tablespoon dried rosemary
1 teaspoon dried sage
1 teaspoon dried basil
1 teaspoon dried oregano
2 bay leaves crushed
1/2 teaspoon dried thyme
1/2 teaspoon garlic granules

Stir together and place in a salt grinder.   Store up to 1 year in a glass jar with a tight fitting lid.

Tuscan Blend Sea Salt

The juniper berries have a slightly smoky flavor that gives a meaty flavor to eggplant, mushrooms and tofu. This blend also enhances roasted or steamed veggies, tomato sauce, salads, soups and stews with an Italian flair.
Yield – 2/3 cup

1/2 cup coarse sea salt
1 tablespoon Italian Seasoning Blend
1 rounded teaspoon red pepper flakes
1 teaspoon garlic granules
2 teaspoons juniper berries

Stir together and place in a salt grinder. Store up to 1 year in a glass jar with a tightly fitting lid.

 # GF Pastry Flour Blend

I tend to use Gluten Free Mama's Almond Flour Blend in much of my baking, but since it is not available in many parts of the country and it does contain nuts, here is a nut free option that is a great substitute especially for cakes. Most GF flours are simply starches without fiber or much nutritional value. The addition of nutritional yeast to this blend introduces valuable vitamins and minerals. This is my version of an "enriched" pastry style flour.
Yield – 3 cups

1 cup superfine brown rice flour
2/3 cup potato starch
1/2 cup sweet brown rice flour
2/3 cup tapioca flour
1 teaspoon nutritional yeast powder
1 3/4 teaspoon guar or xanthan gum

If you can only find nutritional yeast in flakes, grind in a spice grinder or small food processor until it forms a powder. Using a fine mesh sifter, sift ingredients 4 times. Store in an airtight glass jar in a dark, cool place.

GF Bean and Seed Flour Blend

This blend utilizes ground beans and seeds making it a bit more like a whole grain flour. It is much higher in protein, fiber and minerals than traditional GF blends. Since the beans and seeds in this recipe have fairly strong flavors, I like to use it with other strong flavors like pumpkin, banana and maple. Try it when baking a loaf of yeast bread for a nutty flavor.
Yield – 6 cups

3/4 cup garbanzo bean flour
3/4 cup fava bean flour
1/4 cup sorghum flour
1/4 cup teff flour
1/2 cup potato starch
 1 3/4 cups tapioca flour
1 3/4 cups organic cornstarch

Triple sift and store in a glass jar with a tightly fitting lid in a cool, dark place.

Kitchen Tip: Because flours contain naturally occurring oils, you can extend their freshness by storing in the freezer. Just be sure to bring it up to room temperature before adding to your recipe.

Spice Blends

To make the best spice blends use a coffee grinder specifically designated for spices. Measure, mix then grind all ingredients to release their aromatic oils. To keep your blends at their best, make small batches, store in airtight glass containers in a cool dark place. Just before using lightly toast them in a small skillet until their aroma becomes intense or pop them in your spice grinder for a few turns. Either method encourages the herbs and spices to release more aromatic oils resulting in more flavor.

Chai Spice Blend

The aroma from this mix is so sweet and earthy that you will be dreaming up all kinds of ways to use this blend, from fruit tortes to apple cider to spiced wine and even yams. Add a little to your East Indian Curry to create a dish with more complex flavors. This one is so useful I've repeated it from my first cookbook.
Yield – 1/3 cup

2 tablespoons cinnamon
1 tablespoon ginger
2 teaspoons nutmeg
1 1/2 teaspoon cloves
1 1/2 teaspoons allspice
1 teaspoon cardamom
1 teaspoon dried orange zest
1/4 teaspoon cracked black pepper
1/2 vanilla bean

I prefer to grind my own cinnamon, cloves, cardamom, grate my own nutmeg and grind my own pepper because it tastes and smells so much better. To grind cinnamon break 1-2 sticks into smaller pieces and grind in a spice

or coffee grinder. Orange peel is not always easy to find, so simply zest a couple of oranges and cut into 1/2 inch pieces. Dehydrate then grind into powder. I generally store mine in pieces then grind as I need it. Put all spices in a bowl, whisk to full incorporate then quickly grind in a coffee or spice grinder. Place spices in a jar or tin with an airtight lid. Slice the vanilla pod lengthwise and push it into the spices. In a few days the entire mix will meld.

Cuban Spice Blend

This is a really great mix I designed to provide the warm spices along with the heat of chilies that is so intoxicating in Cuban dishes. Try it to season black beans, rice, chicken, fish and tofu. Another repeat from my first cookbook!

Yield – 1/2 cup

2 teaspoons Celtic sea salt
1 tablespoon cumin
1 tablespoon ground ginger
1 tablespoon coriander
1 tablespoon cinnamon
1 1/2 teaspoon garlic powder
1 1/2 tsp fennel
1 teaspoon cayenne
1 teaspoon black pepper
1 1/2 teaspoon allspice
3/4 teaspoon cloves
3/4 teaspoon red pepper flakes

Place all ingredients in a spice grinder and process until completely combined. Store in a glass jar up to 6 months.

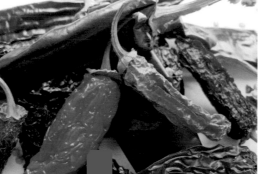

Bruschetta Spice Blend

Sprinkle over goat cheese, on top of steaming pasta, over warm buttered bread, over ripe tomatoes or your favorite salad - and this is just the beginning of what you can dream up to use this handy blend of the best if Italy . . .
Yield – 1/4 cup

3 sundried tomatoes – not packed in oil – finely minced
1 tablespoon garlic granules
2 tablespoons Italian seasoning
1 teaspoon red pepper flakes
2 teaspoons Celtic sea salt

Add all ingredients to a spice grinder and pulse until tomatoes are fine and herbs are well mixed. Store in a container with a tightly fitting lid. Keeps 6-9 months in a dark, cool place.

 # Hot and Spicy Citrus Blend

This blend is perfect to add a hint of Mexico to your favorite dishes. To dry zest simply zest your citrus fruit place on a kitchen towel and air dry for 24-48 hours or place in a dehydrator approximately 8 hours.
Yield – 1/4 cup

1 teaspoon sweet paprika
1/4 teaspoon smoked paprika
1/2 teaspoon cumin
1/8 teaspoon cayenne
1/8 teaspoon pasilla pepper
1/8 teaspoon chipotle pepper
1/4 teaspoon dried cilantro
¼ teaspoon red chili flakes

1 teaspoon Celtic sea salt
1/4 teaspoon freshly ground black pepper
1/4 teaspoon garlic granules
1/4 teaspoon dry lemon zest
1/4 teaspoon dry lime zest
1/8 teaspoon Mexican oregano

Pulse in a spice grinder until fragrant and completely blended. Store in a small glass jar with a tight fitting lid. Store in a dark, cool place up to 9 months.

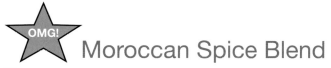 ## Moroccan Spice Blend

This is a spicy, deeply red North African spice blend that is perfect to season chickpea stews, couscous and rice dishes. Yield – 1/4 cup

1 tablespoon ground cumin
1 teaspoon ground coriander
1 teaspoon ancho chile powder
1 teaspoon sweet paprika
1/2 teaspoon ground cinnamon
1/2 teaspoon Celtic sea salt
1/4 teaspoon smoked paprika
1/4 teaspoon ground allspice
1/4 teaspoon ground ginger
1/8 teaspoon cayenne pepper
1/8 teaspoon ground cloves

Pulse in a spice grinder and store in a small glass jar with a tightly fitting lid. This blend will keep 6-9 months in a dark, cool place.

★ OMG! Spicy Mustard and Pepper Blend

This is a great spice blend to add a kick to plain mayo, olive oil, butter or hollandaise sauce, artichokes and asparagus.
Yield – about 2 tablespoons

1 1/2 teaspoon sweet paprika
3/4 teaspoon cumin
1/4 teaspoon cayenne pepper
1 teaspoon dry mustard
1/4 teaspoon red pepper flakes
1/2 teaspoon granulated garlic
1 teaspoon Celtic sea salt

Pulse in a spice grinder and store in a jar with a tight fitting lid in a dark, cool place up to 9 months.

Sweet Fall Spice Blend

This is such a useful blend and replaces traditional pumpkin pie spice that you can purchase in most grocery stores. It is terrific in pumpkin, sweet potato, apple and pear dishes. For a much more fragrant and tasty version, try making your blend with whole spices. In a spice or coffee grinder mix the following in small batches until the powder is fine. The aroma alone will intoxicate you. Below you will find the measurements for a quick version using ground spices and a version using whole spices.

4 large cinnamon sticks, broken into 1/2 inch pieces
1 teaspoon whole cloves
1 rounded teaspoon allspice berries
1/4 whole nutmeg
1 tablespoon ground ginger

Mix together and store in a glass container with a tightly fitting lid. This is so wonderful when absolutely fresh but can be stored for 6 months. To revitalize simply grind again for 30 seconds to release oils once again.

Ginger Paste

Ginger paste is such a simple way to layer flavors in your dishes in no time. It takes just a few minutes to prepare and like pesto or grilled peppers, the secret to a longer shelf life is creating an olive oil barrier to retard bacterial growth. So each time you use some paste, just be sure the remaining paste is level and covered with oil. Since ginger is one of those fresh spices that tends to either dry out or get moldy if you don't use them quickly enough, this not only saves you time, but it also saves you money!
Yield – 1/4 cup thick paste

1/4 cup ginger, peeled then sliced
1 teaspoon Celtic sea salt
Olive oil to cover

Peel ginger using a spoon. This is the fastest way to remove the peel while retaining most of the flesh. Place in food processor and process until you get a creamy, thick paste. Scrape into a small jar, top with a quarter inch of olive oil to create the barrier, top with a tightly fitting lid and store in the refrigerator for up to 3 months . . . mine never lasts that long!

Garlic Paste

Making garlic paste is the single easiest way to save lots of time in the kitchen. It's quick, easy and lasts up to 3 weeks. A very thick layer of olive oil retards bacterial growth while providing very flavorful garlic oil.
Yield – 1/3 cup thick paste

1/3 cup garlic, peeled
1 tablespoon Celtic sea salt
2 tablespoons olive oil + more to cover

The fastest way to peel garlic is to smash it with the broad side of a chef's knife. This releases the peel from the garlic clove. Place in food processor with salt and 2 tablespoons oil and process until you get a creamy, thick paste. Scrape into a small jar, top with a half inch of olive oil to create the barrier, top with a tightly fitting lid and store in the refrigerator for up to 3 weeks.

Preserved Citrus Fruit

Preserved lemons are a staple ingredient in Middle-Eastern foods as well as Southeast Asian dishes. Soups and stews generally use the inner flesh while fish and chicken dishes, salads and mezze plates use the rinds, which are also a delicious addition to spicy tomato drinks. Preserved limes, oranges and grapefruit are equally delicious and extremely versatile. These salty fruits are generally rinsed to remove excess salt, but this recipe uses far less salt, so that step is not absolutely necessary. You can also use just a bit of the oil in a salad dressing or marinade if you like.
Yield – 1 pint jar

The same technique and proportions are used no matter which fruit you are preserving, so this recipe uses lemons but you can substitute limes, tangerines, oranges or small ruby red grapefruit. In fact since blood oranges, Meyer's lemons and limes are only available for short periods of time each year, this is a terrific way to extend their life.

3 medium sized organic lemons
1/2 cup freshly squeezed lemon juice
1 tablespoon Celtic sea salt
Olive oil to cover

Cut lemons into quarters and roll in 2 teaspoons of the salt and place in a bowl. Pour lemon juice into a sterilized pint jar. Layer lemons, remaining salt, and juices that the lemons have given up into the jar, pressing them down as you go, then cover completely with olive oil. Sit on counter for 24-36 hours before refrigerating. Refrigerate 3 weeks before using.

Each time you use a lemon, be certain that the remaining fruit is covered with oil, adding more if necessary.

Grilled Preserved Lemons with Thyme

These are so easy to prepare and provide so much flavor that I think you will be absolutely hooked! You can use them in any savory dish to add a pop of smoky, lemony flavor. Preserved lemons are a staple ingredient in Middle-Eastern foods as well as Southeast Asian dishes. Soups and stews generally use the inner flesh while fish and chicken dishes, salads and mezze plates use the rinds, which are also a delicious addition to spicy tomato drinks. They are generally rinsed to remove excess salt, but this recipe uses far less salt, so that step is not absolutely necessary. You can also use just a bit of the oil in a salad dressing or marinade if you like.
Yield – 1 pint jar

3 medium sized organic lemons
1/2 cup freshly squeezed lemon juice
5 teaspoons Celtic sea salt
4 sprigs fresh thyme
Olive oil to cover

Heat your grill to a medium temperature. Cut lemons in half, brush with a bit of olive oil and grill, cut side down, until lemons have softened and charred grill marks appear. This step concentrates the lemon flavor as well as adding a smoky flavor from the caramelized sugars. Pour lemon juice into a sterilized pint jar. Place lemons in a pint jar, layering with salt and thyme, cover completely with olive oil. Sit on counter for 24 hours before refrigerating. Refrigerate 3 weeks before using. Each time you use a lemon, be certain that the remaining fruit is covered with oil, adding more if necessary.

Flavor Combinations

Here are some options I really like. Feel free to come up with your own.

Pair grilled limes with 1 teaspoon red chili flakes
Pair blood oranges with basil and Hawaiian red salt
Pair tangerines with sage and Himalyan pink salt

Follow all of the instructions in the previous recipes. Remember the time the fruit sits at room temperature is essential in the development of both prebiotics and probiotics and when combined with the high Vitamin C content these are a great immune booster!

Southwestern Style Spicy Pickled Veggies

These are zippy pickles, and it's hard to get enough of them! Use the veggies whole on a cheese tray, slice to use as a spicy veggie garnish, or add to an otherwise plain tossed salad or serve with your favorite grilled entrée for an extra kick. Yield – 1 pint jar

Pack a clean sterilized jar with an assortment from the following list of veggies:
Whole spicy fresh peppers – jalapeno, serrano, or small poblano
Baby carrots or carrot sticks
Onions – whole pearl or wedges of red or yellow
Bell peppers – small whole red, yellow or orange or thick slices
Young green beans
Okra
Sundried or oven dried tomatoes

Add the following:
4 whole garlic cloves
2 sprigs Mexican oregano
4 sprigs cilantro
1/4 teaspoon cumin
1/4 teaspoon whole mustard seeds
1/4 teaspoon chipotle chili powder
3/4 teaspoon Celtic sea salt
Spicy Southwestern Vinegar to cover – about 1 cup

In a small non-reactive pan heat vinegar, salt and dry spices, stirring occasionally until salt has dissolved. Remove from heat and cool to 100 degrees or less to preserve the naturally occurring enzymes. Spoon spices into jar and pour in enough vinegar to completely cover the veggies. Cap tightly and sit on counter for 24-36 hours then refrigerate at least 3 weeks to allow veggies to pickle. Feel free to reuse this flavored pickling vinegar as the base for more pickled veggies or in a spicy vinaigrette.

Entertainment Tip: Use this pickling liquid to rim a glass before dipping in salt for spicy juices or cocktails.

⭐ OMG! Spicy Dilled and Pickled Veggies

Making your own fresh pickles is a great way to take advantage of beautiful and abundant produce, reduce the salt content and make varieties you cannot find at your local market. These pickled veggies are made in the refrigerator so no special equipment is needed. They are a bit spicy from the peppers, crisp and tart with that wonderfully fresh flavor only dill can impart. The colors remain a bit brighter than processed pickles; the natural enzymes in the veggies are enhanced so they naturally improve digestion. So add a few whole pieces as a garnish, chop and include in salads or serve on your next cheese tray. It's such a great way to preserve the fresh produce of summer and they make a welcomed hostess gift.
Yield – 1 pint jar

Pack a clean and sterilized jar with your own favorite assortment of veggies from this list:
Small whole bell peppers or thick slices of red, yellow or orange
Small pickling cucumbers
Baby zucchini or yellow squash
Okra
Young green beans
Whole sugar snap or snow peas
Shallots or pearl onions
Cauliflower or broccoli florettes

Add the following:
3 whole garlic cloves
3 sprigs dill
1 bay leaf
1 small dried hot chile pepper
1/4 teaspoon whole mustard seeds
1/4 teaspoon celery seeds
3/4 teaspoon Celtic sea salt
Dilled Vinegar to cover – about 1 cup depending upon how tightly the veggies are packed

In a small saucepan heat the vinegar, salt and dried spices, stirring occasionally until salt dissolves. Cool to below 100 degrees. Spoon spices into jar and pour in enough vinegar to completely cover. Cap tightly then set on counter for 24-36 hours. Refrigerate for at least 3 weeks before eating to allow veggies to properly cure.

Kitchen Tip - Pickling liquid can be reused to make more pickled veggies, in marinades and vinaigrettes.

★ OMG! Fire Roasted Peppers

I love roasted peppers . . . sweet, smoky, tender, colorful and simple to make . . . what's not to love? During the late summer and fall they are available and inexpensive at local farm stands and markets. It's a great time to stock up and preserve a few. I store some in the refrigerator and more in the freezer for winter and use them in so many ways to add a pop of color, flavor and tons of Vitamins C and A.

1 each red, yellow and orange bell peppers (or use all 1 color)
3 cloves garlic cut in half
6-8 large basil leaves
Olive oil to cover

Roast peppers over an open flame (or under broiler), turning as necessary until charred on all sides. Place in a glass bowl with a tight fitting lid 5-10 minutes. This creates a pocket of steam that further separates the skin from the flesh of the peppers. At this point the skins will peel off in large strips. Place a mesh strainer over a bowl and hold peppers over the bowl to catch juices while you cut peppers in half to remove stem and seeds. Pack peppers into a bowl or jar with a tight fitting lid, alternating colors, and adding basil and garlic with each layer. Pour juices over peppers, then add enough olive oil to cover completely.

Refrigerated, these will keep about 6 weeks, just be certain all peppers are completely covered by oil.   When freezing be certain to leave 1 inch of head room at the top of the jar or bowl as the peppers freeze they expand. Frozen they will keep up to 1 year.

★ OMG! Roasted Garlic

Roasting garlic transforms it into a soft, mellow and nutty spreadable addition to dressings and marinades, main dishes, veggies as well as thick slices of crusty bread.

2 heads garlic
1/3 cup olive oil

Place whole garlic heads in a small ceramic baking dish with a lid. Cover with oil and bake overnight on your oven's lowest setting. Remove from oven and store in refrigerator. Once garlic is gone use the oil to add lots of flavor to sautés, stir fries and much more!

FLAVORED NUTS

Some foods are simply nutritional power houses and nuts and seeds are among them. In my first cookbook, OMG! That's Allergy Free, Vol 1, I included many recipes for candied nuts and seeds inspired by flavors all around the world. So in this volume I've included a simple candied nut recipe plus several recipes for savory nuts and chickpeas. Just like the wonderful candied varieties, these make wonderful addtions to salads, or use 3 or 4 different varieties in small bowls as an appetizer, or pack them in small containers and stick them in your lunch bag, purse or briefcase as a quick, nutritious snack.

 ## Basic Candied Nuts

This treatment can transform your favorite nuts into crunchy, sweet and slightly salty treats. Any nut will work in this recipe and they can be grouped into mounds of chewy, nutty candy clusters, or spread out into individual nuts, so let your imagination run wild!
Yield – 2 1/4 cups

1 teaspoon black strap molasses
1 tablespoon agave nectar
1/3 cup brown rice syrup
1 tablespoon coconut oil
1 teaspoon roasted nut oil, i.e., pistachio, pecan, walnut or pumpkin seed
1 teaspoon good quality vanilla extract
2 cups raw nuts

Bring molasses, agave and rice syrup to a boil. Stirring constantly boil for about 1 minute, add oils and continue to boil for approximately 2 more minutes. Remove from heat and add vanilla and nuts. Stir to coat nuts evenly.

Working quickly, spread out on parchment paper and cool. Store in a parchment lined tin or glass container with a tightly fitting lid.

Rosemary Pecans

I think that rosemary is one of those herbs that pairs well with so many sweet and savory dishes. It is a relative of pine trees so it adds a woodsy overtone to food. Since pecans are rather delicately flavored nuts, this combo is so delicious!
Yield – 2 cups

2 cups pecan halves
3 tablespoons lightly beaten egg whites or flax seed gel
1 teaspoons salt
3/4 teaspoon dried rosemary

Preheat the oven to 225°.

Place nuts in a shallow bowl and toss with egg whites or flax seed gel. This provides a coating for the nuts so the salt and rosemary will cling to the surface. Spread the pecan halves on a large rimmed baking sheet. Since you are using dried rosemary, crush with salt in a mortar and pestle or rub between the palms of your hands to release the oils. Sprinkle evenly across the pecans.

Bake about 45 minutes, or until they appear toasted and coating is set. Cool completely then store in a glass jar with a tight fitting lid.

Sweet and Savory Italian Style Walnuts

A nice addition to salads, these nutritious little nuggets also make great snacks!
Yield - 2 cups

2 cups walnut halves
3 tablespoons lightly beaten egg whites or flax seed gel
1 tablespoon brown rice syrup
1 teaspoons salt
3/4 teaspoon dried rosemary

Follow directions for Rosemary Pecans.

CRISPY GARBONZO BEANS

I am a big proponent of layering flavors in salads by adding spiced nuts. However, a great alternative to spiced nuts are crunchy, flavored garbanzo beans . . . their unique nutritional profile makes them an excellent choice when you want a low fat option to nuts!

Basic Instructions:

Preheat oven to 375 degrees. Lightly spray a rimmed baking sheet with organic olive oil. Drain, rinse and pat dry a can of organic garbanzo beans then place in a bowl. Spray with organic olive oil just enough to coat the beans. Sprinkle the seasonings and salt over the beans and mix well. Spread on baking sheet in a single layer and bake about 40 minutes or until crisp and lightly browned. Cool completely then store in a glass container with a tightly fitting lid to retain crisp texture.

Crunchy Chile Lime Chickpeas

1 14 ounce can organic garbanzo beans
1/4 teaspoon garlic granules
1 pinch teaspoon cayenne pepper
1/4 teaspoon chili powder
1/4 teaspoon Celtic sea salt
Olive Oil Spray

Chickpeas Havana Style

1 14 ounce can organic garbanzo beans
1/2 teaspoon Cuban Spice Blend
1/4 teaspoon Celtic sea salt
Olive Oil Spray

Crispy Italian Style Garbanzos

1 14 ounce can organic garbanzo beans
1/2 teaspoon Bruschetta Spice Blend
1/4 teaspoon Celtic sea salt
Olive Oil Spray

Compound Butters, Sauces and Gravies

What if you could magically transform ordinary veggies into taste temping delights by adding only a single ingredient? That is the magic of compound butters. You make them, wrap and freeze them for months and simply slice off a piece, and just that fast you go from ordinary to extraordinary veggies, rice and pasta!

Sauces can make some plain pasta and veggies into a beautiful meal or some grilled polenta into a quick pizza. They can turn a serving of fish, chicken or tofu into something spectacular by adding just a little dollop or drizzle. And what hollandaise can do for a simple poached egg or tofu scramble is the magic legendary meals are made of.

Gravy . . . ahhhhh, gravy . . . the crown jewel of comfort foods . . . Who knew that silky, sumptuous gravy could actually be a healthy source of vitamins, minerals and even fiber?

So put your chef's hat on and make some magic!

Ultra Creamy 5 Cheese Sauce

This sauce is a combo of intensely flavored goat and sheep's milk cheeses that produce the best cheese sauce! It's velvety smooth, wonderfully complex flavor with a decadent feel. Try it with pasta for a terrific mac and cheese, with potatoes for a decadent gratin or over drizzle over steamed veggies.
Yield – 2 ½ cups

1 ounce Roqufort cheese crumbles
1 ounce pecorino cheese shredded
1 1/2 ounces goat's milk mozzarella shredded
2 ounces fresh goat cheese crumbled
1 ounce Romano cheese shredded
1 tablespoon butter
1 tablespoon pistachio oil
1/2 teaspoon
2 cups unsweetened soy milk
2 tablespoons white spelt or Mama's GF Almond Blend + 1/4 teaspoon xanthan gum
1 teaspoon white pepper
1/8 teaspoon nutmeg

Melt butter and oil in a heavy bottomed 2 quart pan. Add flour and thoroughly combine, stirring constantly, cooking until it just before it starts to brown. Reduce heat and whisk in soy milk, stirring until it begins to thicken. Add cheese a little at a time whisking to completely incorporate after each addition. Add pepper and nutmeg, taste and adjust seasonings.

 Fire Roasted Poblano and Cilantro Pesto

This is a fantastic pesto! A little spicy from the jalapeno, slightly smoky from the roasted poblanos, fragrant from the cilantro, bright flavor from the lime, nutty from the toasted almonds and pumpkin seeds and a little salty from the manchego . . . it's unlike any pesto you have ever tasted! It's fantastic tossed with pasta, as a spread on crostinis, mixed with Sour Crème Substitute or Lemonaise as a dip for fresh veggies, and so much more! I suggest making more than you need so you can keep it on hand in the refrigerator.
Yield – 1 1/4 cups

1/3 cup toasted almonds
2 tablespoons raw pumpkin seeds
4 cloves roasted garlic
1 1/2 teaspoons diced jalapeno
1 cup roasted and diced poblano peppers (about 2)
1 1/2 cup cilantro leaves and tender stems
1 teaspoon red chili flakes
2 tablespoons lime juice
1/4 teaspoon each, Celtic sea salt and black pepper
1/3 cup finely grated manchego cheese
1/4 cup Lime Infused Olive Oil + more for topping

In the bowl of your food processor add almonds, pumpkin seeds, garlic, jalapeno and cilantro and process until almonds are in very small pieces. Add remaining ingredients, except oil, and process until smooth. Stream the olive oil in while processor is running.
Spoon into a glass jar or bowl, cover with a layer of olive oil until completely covered, top with a tight fitting lid and refrigerate.

Each time you use some pesto be certain that the remainder is completely covered with oil. The oil acts as a barrier and keeps pesto fresh for 2 months or more.

 ## Sundried Tomato Pesto

The concentrated sweet flavors from sundried tomatoes, the heady aroma of fresh basil, and the earthy flavor of roasted garlic are the essence of Tuscan cooking . . . This pesto is so rich and smooth and delicious no one would guess that it's loaded with

antioxidants, vitamins and minerals. It is equally delicious with sheep's milk Romano or nut cheeze so experiment to see which you prefer. Just 1 tablespoon will elevate an ordinary tomato sauce to extraordinary heights! Try it on grilled No Knead Splet Ciabatta slices, grilled eggplant sandwiches or mix into Basic Mayo for a really great spread or dip.
Yield – 1 3/4 cups

1/4 cup pine nuts
1 1/4 cup basil leaves
3 cloves Roasted Garlic
1/3 cup sundried tomatoes packed in oil
1/3 cup grated Romano or Cashew Goat Cheeze
1 1/2 teaspoons nutritional yeast
1/4 teaspoon red chili flakes
2 teaspoons lemon juice
1/4 teaspoon Tuscan Blend Sea Salt
3 tablespoons Basil Infused Olive Oil
3 tablespoons Sundried Tomato Infused Olive Oil
1/4 teaspoon freshly ground coarse black pepper

Place all ingredients except oil in the bowl of a food processor and pulse until smooth. Next turn unit on and slowly add 2 tablespoons of each oil and process until smooth. If the mixture is too thick add up to 2 tablespoons pH 11.5 ionized water.

Place in a small wide mouthed glass jar and cover the top with remaining oil. Store tightly capped in the refrigerator. Be certain that the top is always covered in oil to retard spoilage.

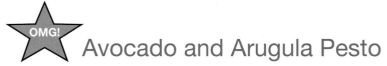 ## Avocado and Arugula Pesto

This is a Mexitalian pesto sauce . . . peppery arugula, creamy avocado, lime, basil, cumin and cilantro all combine to create a delicious sauce that is packed with essential fatty acids, calcium, magnesium, potassium and protein. It's great tossed with pasta, added to salad, served with blue corn chips or crackers or blended with Sour Crème Substitute or Basic Blender Mayonnaise as a fresh veggie dip.
Yield – 1 1/2 cups

1/4 cup toasted almonds
1 1/2 cup firmly packed baby arugula
1 cup basil leaves
1/2 cup avocado (1 small avocado)
2 cloves garlic or 1 teaspoon garlic paste
2 tablespoons chopped cilantro
2 tablespoons lime juice
1/4 cup Romano finely grated or
Feta Cheeze Crumbles
1/8 teaspoon cumin
1/4 teaspoon red pepper flakes
Salt and Pepper to taste
2 tablespoons extra virgin olive oil

Place all ingredients in the bowl of your food processor and pulse a few times, then process until smooth and creamy. This pesto is best used within 24 hours.

Almond and Arugula Pesto

OMG!

You can make this one with or without cheese and it is simply delicious. The peppery arugula provides a very nice background for the sweet basil, while the toasted almonds and olive oil provide a very creamy finish to this delicious and very affordable pesto. I like to add a little salty Pecorino cheese to balance out the peppery arugula, but nut cheeze works well for a vegan option. Try it both ways!
Yield – 1 1/4 cups

1/2 cup toasted almonds
1/2 teaspoon lemon zest
3 tablespoons lemon juice
2 cups baby arugula leaves
1 cup fresh basil leaves
1 teaspoon garlic paste or 2 cloves grated garlic
1/4 cup finely grated Pecorino cheese or Feta Cheeze Crumbles
1/4 teaspoon Celtic sea salt
1/4 teaspoon freshly grated black pepper
1/3 cup olive oil

Place all ingredients, except olive oil, in the bowl of your food processor. Pulse a few times then process until you have achieved a thick paste. Slowly stream the oil in through the tube and process until it is completely incorporated.
To store for later use, spoon into a glass jar, pressing down and smoothing to get most of the air pockets out. Top with a 1/4 inch layer of olive oil. This locks the air away and acts as a barrier to bacteria and mold. Each time you use some of the pesto, simply smooth it out and top with a little more oil if necessary.

Green Chimichurri Sauce and Marinade

Chimichurri is a terrific sauce or marinade that originated in Argentina. It's a very fresh, herbaceous, slightly spicy sauce with a refreshing minty overtone. This variety is a perfect marinade for meats, seafood, poultry and tofu.
Yield – 1 cup

1/2 cup lightly toasted pepitas
1 cup Italian parsley leaves roughly chopped
1/2 cup cilantro leaves
1/4 cup mint leaves
4 cloves roasted garlic
2 teaspoons nutritional yeast
1/4 cup diced red onion
1 1/2 teaspoons crushed red pepper
1 teaspoon each sea salt and black pepper
1 tablespoon red wine vinegar
1/4 cup olive oil
2 tablespoons pumpkin seed oil

Place all leaves, garlic, onion, and seasonings in a food processor and pulse until finely chopped. Add vinegar and process until a sauce begins to form then stream in olive oil and that is it!

Red Chimichurri Sauce and Marinade

Chimichurri sauce is the Argentinean version of pesto. This particular sauce is a bit spicier than Green Chimichurri and creates such a spicy finish to all meat, fish, poultry and tofu dishes as well as grilled tropical fruit as a surprise.
Yield – 1/2 cup

1 tablespoon crushed red pepper
2 teaspoons chipotle peppers in adobo sauce
3/4 cup Italian parsley leaves
1/4 cup fresh oregano leaves
2 cloves diced garlic
2 tablespoons finely diced red onion
1/2 teaspoon Celtic sea salt
1 tablespoon red wine vinegar
3/4 teaspoon smoked paprika
3 tablespoons olive oil

Traditionally this would be prepared in a mortar and pestle, but you can make it in a food processor if you like.

Blender Hollandaise Sauce

Repeated from my first cookbook by popular demand! I'll let you in on a little secret, chefs are secretly intimidated by hollandaise sauce. It breaks so easily—just a little too much heat, or a little too much or too little whisking (or even if you look at it with a scowl) and it separates. But this recipe has never, ever failed me! So when you are ready for a rich, creamy, buttery, slightly tangy topping for your fish or asparagus or eggs . . . well here's the recipe for you!
Yield – 1 cup

3 egg yolks
4 tsp freshly squeezed lemon juice
2 tablespoons ph 11.5 ionized water, boiling
1 cup very warm melted butter
1 dash cayenne pepper
Celtic sea salt to taste

Place the egg yolks in the VitaMix and process on level 4, very slowly add the boiling water. In a slow steady stream, add the butter. Increase speed to level 6 and add the lemon juice, cayenne and salt. Taste and adjust the seasonings.

Vegan Hollandaise Sauce

This version of hollandaise is smooth and creamy like its egg filled counterpart, yet it still is maintains the silky and lemony flavors. Enjoy it over asparagus, broccoli and cauliflower or vegan eggs benedict.
Yield – 1 1/2 cups

6 ounces silken tofu
1/4 cup Veganaise
1/4 cup Herb Infused Olive Oil
1/4 cup Lemon Infused Olive Oil
3 cloves roasted garlic
3 tablespoons lemon juice
3 tablespoons unsweetened soy milk
1 rounded teaspoon Dijon mustard
1/8 teaspoon turmeric powder
1/8 teaspoon Celtic sea salt
1/4 teaspoon white pepper
1 dash cayenne pepper

Using a VitaMix or other powerful blender, combine ingredients in order. Blend until smooth. Taste and adjust salt and pepper to taste.

 # Roasted Red Pepper and Sundried Tomato Dip

This is a smooth, creamy and very flavorful dip for veggies, spread for crackers or bread, or use it as a creamy tomato pasta sauce. Versatile, quick to prepare and so delicious, with hints of the smoky goodness from the fire roasted peppers . . . all of that and it's also guilt free since it's packed with healthy sources of essential fatty acids, high levels of lycopene, trace minerals and even protein.
Yield – 1 1/2 cups

1/2 cup coarsely chopped, Fire Roasted Red Bell Peppers
1 tablespoon Sundried Tomato Infused Olive Oil
1 tablespoon Sundried Tomato Vinegar
1/4 cup toasted almonds

2 large cloves Roasted Garlic or 1 1/2 teaspoons Garlic Paste
1/2 cup basil leaves
1/4 to 1/2 teaspoons red pepper flakes
1/2 cup sundried tomatoes
2 tablespoons Basic Mayonnaise or Veganaise
1/2 cup Crème Cheese Substitute or Goat Cheeze
Celtic sea salt and freshly ground black pepper to taste

In the bowl of your food processor, combine peppers, olive oil, almonds, garlic, basil, red pepper flakes and tomatoes. Pulse or process until smooth then add mayo and Ricotta Substitute and pulse until combined. Transfer to a serving bowl and garnish with a few pieces of sundried tomato slices and a sprig of basil, or toss with steamed veggies or pasta. Refrigerate up to 2 weeks, treat like pesto and cover with a thin layer of olive oil.

Basic Blender Mayonnaise

 When I learned to make mayo it required about 20 minutes of hand whisking and the consistency was a bit thin. But this mayo could not possibly be easier or faster to make. Using an immersion blender takes all of the work out of the process and the end result is thick, creamy and delicious . . .
Yield 1 cup.

1 fresh organic egg
2 tsp stone ground dijon mustard
2 tsp ph 9.5 ionized water
2 tbs freshly squeezed lemon juice*
1/4 tsp Celtic sea salt
1/4 tsp xanthan gum
1 tsp agave
2/3 cup olive oil

In the container that came with your immersion blender, or in a 2 cup glass measuring cup, break the egg in the bottom, add all the remaining ingredients adding oil last. Place the blender at the bottom of the cup and blend for about 15-20 seconds. Then lift the blender 2-3 times and continue to blend until ingredients are fully incorporated and mayo is thick. Refrigerate and use within 1 week.

Easy Mayo Upgrages

Use the following suggestions to pair a flavor enhanced mayo with your favorite sandwich or creamy salad! To 1 cup mayo add the following and blend until completely incorporated . . . .

Roasted Garlic and Walnut Mayo - add 1 tablespoon roasted walnut oil, 1 tablespoon roasted garlic paste

Wasabi Mayo - add 1 teaspoon wasabi powder and blend very well

Cranberry Orange Mayo - stir in 1 tablespoon orange juice, 1 teaspoon orange zest and 1/4 cup dried cranberries

Dill and Caper Mayo - stir in 1 1/2 teaspoons diced capers and 2 teaspoons chopped fresh dill

Quick And Easy Lemonnaise

This flavored mayo is so good that I use it as a dip for artichokes, asparagus spears, a sauce for broccoli and cauliflower, and the base for some of my favorite salads.
Yield 1 cup

1 fresh organic egg
2 teaspoons stone ground Dijon mustard
2 teaspoons pH 9.5 ionized water
3 tablespoons freshly squeezed lemon juice*
1 teaspoon Herb Infused Vinegar
1 teaspoon agave nectar
1/4 teaspoon Celtic sea salt
1/4 teaspoon xanthan gum
1 teaspoon finely chopped garlic
1/2 teaspoon chopped basil
1/2 teaspoon tarragon
1/4 teaspoon cayenne pepper
1 teaspoon lemon zest
2/3 cup olive oil

In the container that came with your immersion blender, or in a 2 cup glass measuring cup, break the egg in the bottom, add all the remaining ingredients adding oil last.

Place the blender at the bottom of the cup and blend for about 15-20 seconds. Then lift the blender 2-3 times and continue to blend until ingredients are fully incorporated and mayo is thick. Refrigerate and use within 1 week.

 # Chocolate Balsamic Vinegar

This is nothing short of a decadent treat to use on fresh ripe strawberries, raspberries and figs, or as a drizzle over berry ladened shortcakes . . . who knew something so simple could be so outrageously delicious . . .
Yield – 1/2 cup

1 cup good quality balsamic vinegar
1 ounce good quality dark chocolate
1 small pinch guar or xanthan gum

In a small, non-reactive sauce pan bring vinegar to a simmer and cook until reduced by half. Remove from heat and cool until warm but not hot. Add chopped chocolate and guar gum and whisk vigorously until fully incorporated. Pour into a small bottle with a cork or screw top lid.

Compound Butters

As I mentioned in my first cookbook, compound butters are one of the easiest ways to at a wonder layer of flavor to any side dish, from rice and pasta, to veggies, fish, poultry, seafood and tofu, as well as muffins and waffles!

The technique is simple. Bring 1/2 cup butter to room temperature, thoroughly incorporate ingredients, shape into a log, wrap in parchment paper, then a zipper bag and freeze. To use, slice off a piece and set it atop your dish!

Strawberry-Basil Butter - 1 tablespoon fruit sweetened strawberry jam, 1 1/2 teaspoons finely diced basil
Blackberry-Sage Butter - 1 tablespoon fruit sweetened blackberry jam, 1 teaspoon finely chopped sage
Strawberry-Orange Butter - 1 tablespoon fruit sweetened strawberry jam, 1 tablespoon orange juice, 1 teaspoon orange zest
Orange-Ginger Butter - 1 teaspoon ginger paste, 1 tablespoon orange juice, 1 teaspoon orange zest
Rasbenero Butter - 1 tablespoon fruit sweetened raspberry jam, 1/8 teaspoon very finely minced habanero pepper

Cherry Salsa

Washington is famous for its cherries . . . bing, pie, Rainier, Queen Ann . . . there are so many choices. Since I had neighbors with cherry trees I was often gifted with grocery bags full of these delicious fruit treats, so I designed this recipe to take advantage of the bounty. I hope you enjoy this northwest twist on a southwestern dish. It is a terrific blend of colors, flavors, spices, fruits and herbs. Serve with fish, chicken, tofu or chips and you will not be disappointed.
Yield – 2 cups

1 1/4 cups cherries roughly chopped
3 tablespoons torn cilantro
2 tablespoons green onions
1 heaping tablespoon chopped jalapeno
1 heaping tablespoon chopped red onion
¼ cup chopped yellow and/or orange bell pepper
1 teaspoon lime juice
1/2 teaspoon lime zest
1 pinch salt
1/8 tsp each: cumin, chipotle, cayenne and ancho chili powder

Mix all ingredients together, let sit for a few minutes and serve. Refrigerated it will keep for up to a week.

Mango Salsa

Mango salsa is a wonderful combo of flavors . . . sweet and hot, filled with zesty flavors, this is a great accompaniment to fish, chicken, tofu and blue corn chips. If you have never tried a fruity, tropical twist on salsa, be certain to try this one and you will be hooked!
Yield – 2 cups

1 1/2 cups Mango diced into half inch pieces
3 tablespoons torn cilantro
2 tablespoons green onions, thinly sliced
1/4 cup finely diced red and green jalapenos

2 tablespoons finely diced red onion
1/4 cup finely diced red bell pepper
1 teaspoon minced fresh ginger
Juice and zest from 1/2 large lime
1 pinch salt
1/8 tsp each: cumin, chipotle, cayenne and ancho chili powders

Blend ingredients, place in a non-reactive bowl, cover and allow the flavors to meld, refrigerate up to 7 days.

Asian Style Triple Citrus Glaze

This is one of those perfect surprise sauces . . . the citrus provides the tang, the ginger and schezwan peppers the spicy kick and the tamari a deep and complex salty flavor . . . yum! This makes a thick glaze that's perfect for eggplant, bok choi, green beans, fish, chicken or tofu!
Yield – 1/2 cup

3/4 cup freshly squeezed orange juice
1 teaspoon orange zest
1/4 cup lemon juice
1/4 cup lime juice
1 teaspoon ginger paste
1 tablespoon brown rice vinegar
1 teaspoon lemongrass paste (optional)
2 tablespoons wheat free tamari
1 clove garlic grated
3 tablespoons fruit sweetened apricot jam
1/2 teaspoon toasted sesame oil
1 tablespoon Better Than Bouillon Paste
1/4 teaspoon schezwan pepper
1 teaspoon snipped chives, reserved
2 teaspoons chopped cilantro leaves, reserved

In a small sauce pan bring ingredients to a low boil and cook until reduced in half, add fresh herbs. Refrigerated, this will keep for several weeks.

Fresh Tropical Fruit Chutney

This is a fresh and slightly unconventional approach to a traditional Indian relish. While preserving seasonal fruit is a marvelous way to enjoy it throughout the year, using fresh tropical fruit at the peak of its season has marvelous health benefits. Each of these fruits is loaded with fiber, antioxidants and powerful digestive enzymes, not to mention how delicious they are!

Yield – 2 cups

1/4 cup sweet onion shaved
1 clove finely minced garlic
2 teaspoons grated ginger or ginger paste
1/2 teaspoon lemongrass paste (optional)
Zest and juice of 1/2 lime
1 teaspoon Patak's Red Curry Paste
2 tablespoons fruit sweetened apricot jam
1/2 cup finely chopped mango
1/2 cup finely chopped pineapple
1/2 cup finely chopped papaya
1 tablespoon chopped papaya seeds
1/4 cup finely chopped red bell pepper
3 tablespoons chopped cilantro leaves
1/4 teaspoon Celtic sea salt
1 teaspoon red pepper flakes
3 tablespoons coconut milk
1/4 cup chopped raisins

Chop fruit reserving all juices. Toss with papaya seeds, red pepper, cilantro and shaved onion. If you do not have a mandolin you can mince them very finely.

In a small saucepan heat jam, curry paste, fruit liquids, ginger and garlic until melted. Remove from heat and add coconut milk, salt red pepper flakes and raisins. When completely cooled add to fruit mixture. Cover and refrigerate overnight or leave on countertop for 2 hours before serving.

These flavors are the best of East Indian cuisine and this fresh chutney can be used as a dipping sauce, stirred into basmati rice or quinoa for a side salad or served with poppadum.

⭐ OMG! Spicy Tomato Chutney

When I was growing up turning a bounty of fresh veggies into canned delights for the long winter season was simply part of every summer. Through the years much of this tradition has given way to purchasing delicious treats from gormet shops because canning requires a commitment of time and some specialty equipment. But this chutney is made in the oven so there is no need to constantly stir or watch the pot, and it can be frozen rather than canning it, so no special equipment is necessary! It's a great way to take advantage of beautiful heirloom tomatoes that are a bit overripe and is delicious when served as a dipping sauce or as a part of a cheese plate. Make extra as hostess or holiday gifts!
Yield – 9 cups

10 cups roasted tomatoes chopped
1 inch piece fresh ginger root sliced
1 tablespoon crystallized ginger, chopped
6 cloves roasted garlic
1 1/4 cups pitted and chopped dates
3/4 cup Sundried Tomato Vinegar
4 cups diced onions
1/2 cup golden raisins roughly chopped
2 teaspoons Mixed Spice
1 1/2 teaspoons red chili flakes
1/4 teaspoon each paprika and cayenne
2 tablespoons Patak's red curry paste

In a VitaMix or other powerful blender, process 8 cups of the tomatoes, ginger slices, garlic, 1 cup dates and 2 1/2 cups onions until smooth. Place in a large non-reactive baking dish.

Add crystallized ginger, reserved tomatoes, dates and onions, raisins, vinegar, spices and curry paste. In a 300 degree oven, bake uncovered, stirring occasionally until reduced by 1/3 (this will take several hours). At this point the chutney should be quite thick and very fragrant.

To freeze place in 1/2 pint size freezer safe glass containers with tight fitting lids. Frozen it will keep 6 – 9 months.
To can for longer preservation, follow water bath directions. When lids have sealed and jars have cooled, store in a cool dark place up to 3 years.

Roasted Garlic Tahini Sauce

I really like using roasted garlic in tahini sauce.   Roasting garlic transforms the cloves into a sweet, nutty and creamy little nugget of flavor. In this sauce I think the mellow, nuttiness of the roasted garlic works well with the slight bitterness of the tahini and the bright citrus notes of the lemon juice.
Yield – 1/2 cup

3 cloves roasted garlic
1/4 cup tahini
1/4 cup fresh lemon juice
2 tablespoons pH 9.5 ionized water

Using a VitaMix or inversion blender combine ingredients until smooth and creamy. Store in a small jar with a tightly fitting lid up to 2 weeks in the refrigerator.

Spicy "No Peanuts Please" Sauce

With peanut allergies on the rise, this is a great substitution . . . in fact I like it so much better! It keeps several weeks, so you can use it on your favorite rice noodles, eggplant or steamed greens - I even like it on baked yams.
Yield - 1 1/2 cups

1 cup crunchy style almond butter
2 tablespoons WF tamari or coconut liquid aminos
1 1/2 tablespoons each - sesame oil, Ginger Rice Wine Vinegar, Thai Chili Infused Sesame Oil
2 1/2 teaspoons each Ginger Paste and Garlic Paste
1/3 cup chopped cilantro
1 pinch stevia powder
1 tablespoon agave nectar

On low speed mix all ingredients with an electric mixer, add enough pH 9.5 ionized water to thin into a smooth sauce, about 1/3 cup.

 Coconut Marinade

This marinade is slightly sweet, tangy and spicy. It is a great on its own, but perfect for making coconut chicken, tofu, eggplant, halibut or shrimp. The cultures in the yogurt are the secret to creating a tender and juicy end product while the coconut and spices are subtle and delicious.
Yield – 1 cup

3/4 cup organic Thai Kitchen coconut milk
1/4 cup sheep's milk, goat's milk or coconut milk yogurt
1/2 teaspoon lemongrass paste
1/2 teaspoon ginger paste
1/2 teaspoon chili pepper paste
1/4 teaspoon cayenne pepper
Zest and juice of 1 medium lime

Whisk together very well and coat all sides. Place in a glass container with a tight fitting lid. Marinate tofu overnight, chicken and eggplant at least 2 hours to overnight and shrimp or halibut 1 hour.

Chile-Lime Crema

Smooth, spicy, tart and tangy, this is a great accompaniment to fresh or steamed veggies, fish tacos and salads.
Yield - 1/3 cup

2 tablespoons goat, sheep's milk, soy or coconut yogurt, well drained
2 teaspoons chives, snipped
2 teaspoons cilantro chopped
½ teaspoon chili powder
2 teaspoons lime juice
1 teaspoon lime zest
2 tablespoons finely diced red bell pepper
½ teaspoon Garlic Infused Olive Oil

Place all ingredients in a small bowl and whisk until all ingredients are well incorporated.

SALADS, DRESSINGS & MARINADES

Salads can be so much more than the obligatory first course of a meal. A salad can either be a boring plate of greens on a side plate or the sparkling jewel of the entire meal and much of that depends on the greens and how they are dressed.

I used to be intimidated by salad dressings and vinaigrettes . . . who wouldn't be after reading the ingredient list on the bottles! But after making my first vinaigrette I discovered it was so simple and it tasted better than any bottled dressing I'd ever purchased!

My enthusiasm and my confidence grew and I started making marinades – which were essential to creating flavor filled tofu! So put your fears aside and give these recipes a try and before long you will be dreaming up your own impressive creations!

Keep just a few items stocked in your pantry and refrigerator and you can whip up a delicious dressing or marinade in only 2-3 minutes from start to finish. They can be very simple oil and vinegar mixtures or with just a few extra ingredients you can layer flavors to create a complex flavor combo that will make your taste buds explode!

My favorite salad greens are the fresh, organic, mixed baby lettuces as well as baby spinach and peppery arugula, and we can't forget the ultra-crispy hearts of Romaine. Each of them are tender, crisp, and their lacy or textural leaves allow the dressing to cling for the ultimate taste combo of buttery or bitter greens and sweet, spicy or tart dressing.

So here a few of my favorites with the hope that you will try them and your imagination will take flight with new and even better combos . . . enjoy!

Mango Salad

This salad takes less than 5 minutes to make and is so delicious! It's similar to a very chunky salsa. It's a great side salad with Asian or Mexican style food.
Serves 4

2 large ripe mangos diced
1/4 cup diced red onion
1 cup halved cherry tomatoes
Zest of 1/2 lime
2 tablespoons lime juice
1/4 teaspoon cumin powder
1 large pinch salt
1 dash chili powder
2 tablespoons roughly chopped cilantro leaves
4 bibb lettuce leaves

Whisk lime juice, cumin, salt and chili powder. In a medium bowl, toss in mangos, onion, tomatoes and cilantro. Pour dressing over and marinate for 10 minutes to 1 hour.

Place a lettuce leaf on each salad plate. These leaves will resemble a cup. Fill each lettuce cup with mango salad. Garnish with a few strips of lime zest and a sprig of cilantro.

Melon, Fennel and Watercress with Lemon-Mint Vinaigrette

Cool melon, silky, minty vinaigrette, crisp fresh fennel, fresh lemon, buttery pine nuts and peppery watercress create a taste sensation that will leave you feeling refreshed on a hot day . . . simply perfect for friends or family!
Serves 4

2 cups mixed melon balls (honeydew, cantaloupe or gaia)
1 cup shaved or very thinly sliced fennel

4 cups watercress
2 tablespoons pine nuts
2 ounces Honey and Black Pepper Yogurt Cheese or Goat Cheeze Crumbles
¼ cup Lemon and Mint Vinaigrette

Using your mandolin or sharp knife, shave fennel. Place in the bottom of your salad bowl with about half of the vinaigrette. Toss to thoroughly coat. Set aside while you prepare remaining ingredients.

Lightly toast pine nuts and set aside to cool.

Thoroughly wash and spin dry watercress, remove any tough stems. Halve and remove seeds from your favorite chilled melons, using a small melon ball tool, scoop your melon and set aside. Slice or crumble cheese. Zest lemon.

Add watercress to bowl and toss with fennel. Add melon balls and remaining vinaigrette. Gently turn with tongs. Divide among chilled plates, top with cheese and sprinkle with pine nuts and lemon zest. Serve immediately.

Lemon-Mint Vinaigrette

Slightly tart, refreshingly minty, a wonderful dressing for sweet melons, anise flavored fennel and peppery watercress.
Yield – ½ cup

1 1/2 teaspoons Lemon Sugar
2 tablespoons lemon juice
1 tablespoon Lemon Infused Olive Oil
1/4 cup olive oil
1/2 teaspoon Dijon mustard
1/2 teaspoon salt
5 teaspoons finely chopped fresh mint
1 tablespoon finely minced shallot

Using an immersion blender or VitaMix, place all ingredients in the container and blend until completely emulsified. Refrigerate up to 1 week.

Simple Balsamic Vinaigrette

A super simple, "go to" salad dressing that can be used on salads, steamed or grilled veggies.

2-3 tablespoons aged balsamic vinegar
1/3 cup organic extra virgin olive oil
1 tablespoons ph 11.5 ionized water
1 teaspoon Dijon mustard
1 clove garlic, crushed
1/2 teaspoon Celtic sea salt and freshly ground pepper

In a VitaMix or blender add vinegar, garlic, salt, pepper and mustard. Slowly add the oil & water in a stream. Adjust the salt and pepper to taste.

Cabbage and Apple Slaw

This is a quick to make, fresh slaw with very little oil so the flavors shine. Savoy cabbage and finely grated Fuji apple are the main stars of this light and refreshing salad. Serve with seafood, mustard and black pepper encrusted chicken or chicken-apple sausages.
Yield – 2 servings

4 cups thinly sliced savoy cabbage
1 finely grated Fuji apple
2 tablespoons late harvest Riesling vinegar
1 tablespoon apple cider vinegar
1 teaspoon Dijon mustard
1/2 teaspoon fennel seed
1/2 teaspoon black pepper and Tuscan Blend Sea Salt
2 teaspoons walnut oil

Whisk vinegar, mustard, salt, pepper and oil together well. Pour over cabbage and apple. Cover and let stand for at least 1 hour to overnight before serving.

 # Simple Arugula Salad with Lemon Vinaigrette

Sometimes a very simple salad is often the very best partner to a more complicated main dish . . . the peppery arugula and bright lemon juice are perfectly complimented by smooth and fruity olive oil. Best of all it takes only 2 minutes from start to finish!
Serves 4

6 cups baby arugula
1/4 cup each lemon juice and extra virgin olive oil
1/4 teaspoon each garlic granules and freshly ground black pepper
1/2 teaspoon Mediterranean Blend Sea Salt

Pour lemon juice and olive oil, garlic, salt and pepper into the bottom of a large salad bowl and stir to combine. Place arugula on top and toss to coat.

 # Vegan Caesar Dressing

Traditional Caesar uses raw eggs, cheese and anchovies to create a creamy dressing. This version is so great you will never miss any of those ingredients. The mustard, tahini and Cashew Goat Cheeze make it smooth and creamy and the kelp replaces the anchovies for that authentic Caesar flavor.

1/3 cup fresh lemon juice
1 teaspoon each Dijon mustard, tahini and kelp
2 cloves garlic, crushed
3 tablespoons Cashew Goat Cheeze
1/2 cup extra virgin olive oil
Celtic sea salt and freshly ground pepper to taste

Place lemon juice, mustard, tahini, kelp and garlic in the VitaMix and blend until smooth, add cheese and begin streaming oil until completely emulsified. Add salt and pepper to taste.

⭐ OMG! Arugula Salad with Stuffed Figs, Curried Walnuts and Decadent Chocolate Balsamic Vinaigrette

This salad combines peppery baby arugula with flavorful Curried Walnuts, fresh figs stuffed with Mascarpone Substitute and drizzled with the most decadently flavored vinaigrette . . . If you have stocked your pantry with a few basics it takes only seconds to produce a deceptively nutritious salad that tastes completely decadent.

Serves 2 as a main dish and 4 as a salad course

6 cups baby arugula
8 Fresh Figs Stuffed with Mascarpone and Chocolate Balsamic Vinegar
2 fresh figs chopped
1/3 cup Curried Walnuts
3 tablespoons Chocolate Balsamic Vinaigrette
1/3 cup halved and pitted cherries

In a large bowl toss arugula, chopped figs, cherries and vinaigrette. Divide among salad plates, sprinkle with walnuts and garnish with stuffed figs.

Chocolate Balsamic Vinaigrette

This is a wonderfully decadent way to dress a salad . . . this dressing is so rich only a drizzle is necessary. This vinaigrette is also a fantastic drizzle over fresh figs, berries and pilafs . . . let your imagination be your guide.

Yield – 1/3 cup

2 tablespoons Chocolate Balsamic Vinegar
3 tablespoons roasted walnut oil
1/4 teaspoon freshly ground black pepper

Whisk vigorously until completely incorporated. Store in a bottle with a tightly fitting lid.

Nutrition Note: Each of the components in this salad are so nutrient dense that they are considered nutritional stars! When you consider that rugula is rich in calcium, vitamins A, C and K plus foliate, add potassium, magnesium, manganese and iron and you have greens that pack a powerful nutritional punch. Figs are a nutrient dense fruit, high in potassium, calcium, magnesium, copper and manganese as well as fiber! Walnuts are one of the nutritional kings of the nut family since they are high in essential fatty acids, vitamin E, manganese, copper and tryptophan! The brown rice syrup used as a part of their coating is also rich in minerals and the curry spices increase circulation and decrease blood sugar. Chocolate is not only delicious but contains antioxidants and high levels of magnesium. Cherries balance uric acids and vinegar aids digestion. Who knew a salad could do so much?

Shaved Fennel, Honeycrisp Apple, Spicy Pepper and Arugula Salad

This is one of those beautiful salads that you will enjoy with your eyes as much as your taste buds . . . Fennel has long been known to promote digestion, but did you know that it is a very low calorie, low glycemic, high fiber veggie? Paired with crisp apples, peppery arugula, spicy chile de arbol peppers and shaved sheep's milk pecorino, this is likely to become one of your favorites too . . .

2 cups shaved or very thinly sliced fennel bulb
2 cups julienned honeycrisp or granny smith apple
1 ½ cups baby arugula
Zest and juice of 1/2 fresh lemon
1 medium sized red fresno or red jalapeno pepper minced
1 -2 oz shaved pecorino or Black Pepper Goat Cheeze Crumbles
1/3 cup Lemon and Fennel Vinaigrette
Salt and pepper to taste
Fennel fronds

Using a mandoline shave cheese on narrowest setting. Cover and set aside.
Maintain the same setting and shave fennel, place in salad bowl.   Add half of the vinaigrette and allow to marinate while preparing the remainder of the salad.
Change the setting and slice apples about 1/8 inch thick. Recreate a stack and slice through the stack to create apple slices about 1/8 inch thick and ½ inch wide. Immediately sprinkle with fresh lemon juice to set the color.
To your salad bowl, add half the arugula and toss, add remainder of the arugula the apples, diced pepper and vinaigrette. Toss.
To serve, place on long serving plate, sprinkle with shaved cheese and lemon zest.

Lemon and Fennel Vinaigrette

I created this vinaigrette specifically for my Shaved Fennel Salad with Honeycrisp Apples and Spicy Peppers and Arugula, but it is great with any Italian style salad.
Yields 1/2 cup

2 tablespoons late harvest Riesling vinegar or aged white balsamic vinegar
1 teaspoon Dijon mustard

2 tablespoons toasted walnut oil
1 tablespoon Lemon Infused Olive Oil
1 tablespoon finely chopped fennel fronds
½ teaspoon salt
¼ teaspoon pepper
¼ teaspoon fennel seeds

In a small bowl combine Dijon, seasonings and vinegar, slowly add oils whisking vigorously to emulsify. Taste and adjust to your liking. Refrigerate in a jar with a tightly fitting lid. While I always like my salad dressings as fresh as possible, it will keep for about 1 week.

Spicy Balsamic and Mustard Cole Slaw

This is a simple, spicy, vinegar based slaw. It's best when made a few hours ahead of time and allowed to marinate, this produces a slight pickling effect. Serve with your favorite barbeque, sandwiches or fish tacos.
Serves 4

2 cups shredded cabbage
1/2 cup fine julienned strips red bell pepper
3 tablespoons well aged balsamic vinegar
1 tablespoon whole grain country style Dijon mustard
1/2 teaspoon chipotle pepper
1 tablespoon pH 9.5 ionized water

Toss together, cover bowl, set aside for 30 minutes or refrigerate overnight.

Kitchen Tip : When purchasing balsamic vinegar, remember, the longer the vinegar has been aged the richer and smoother the flavor. Look for varieties that have been barrel aged at least 6 years, but the longer the better! My favorite is from Olivers & Co. Their balsamic is so smooth and yummy you can literally just eat it on a spoon! So use more if it's mellow and less if it still has a sharp "bite".

Meyer's Lemon Vinaigrette

This is a bright, dressing for beautiful greens . . . it's like a taste of summer in every bite.
Yield – ½ cup

1/4 cup juice from Meyer's lemons
1/4 cup Lemon Infused Olive Oil
1 teaspoon grated or minced garlic
1 teaspoon Meyers lemon zest
1/2 teaspoon agave nectar
1/4 teaspoon Dijon mustard
1/2 teaspoon fresh thyme leaves
1/4 teaspoon Celtic sea salt and freshly ground pink or green peppercorns

Blend all ingredients in your VitaMix or vigorously whisk in a small bowl. Refrigerate up to 1 week.

 # Roasted Tomato Vinaigrette

Bright, intense and flavorful . . . this is a perfect vinaigrette for summer veggies or a salad that reminds you of summer days.
Yield – 1/2 cup

1 medium sized Roasted Tomato
3 tablespoons Basil Infused Olive Oil
2 tablespoons Italian Style Herbed Vinegar
3 cloves Roasted Garlic
2 teaspoons chopped basil
1/4 teaspoon freshly ground black pepper
1/2 teaspoon Celtic sea salt

In a VitaMix or powerful blender place all ingredients and blend until smooth. Taste and adjust salt and pepper to taste. Refrigerate up to 1 week.

 Ensalada de Papas Rojas

The hot spices in this southwestern potato salad are balanced with slightly sweet Yukon gold potatoes and cool crisp celery. The brilliant red dressing and bright green herbs and kale make this dish as beautiful as it is delicious and nutritious! Serves 4

2 pounds baby Yukon gold potatoes
4 teaspoons Celtic sea salt
4 celery ribs thinly sliced, including leaves
1 medium red onion diced
2 cloves garlic minced
1/4 cup rough chopped cilantro
1/4 cup rough chopped parsley
2 tablespoons chili powder
1 tablespoon smoked paprika
1 teaspoon ground fennel
1 teaspoon ground cumin
1 teaspoon freshly ground black pepper
1 rounded tablespoon country style Dijon mustard
2 tablespoons Spicy Southwestern Vinegar
1/4 cup olive oil
10 cups kale ribbons

Clean potatoes, cook them whole if they are tiny and halve if slightly larger in a pot – cover with cold water and 1 tablespoon salt. (Salting the water produces a well-seasoned cooked potato.) Boil until tender, but be certain not to overcook baby potatoes.

Meanwhile, steam the kale until tender, about 6-8 minutes. Drain well, cover and set aside.

Choose any blend of chili powder you like. I prefer a blend of chipotle, pasilla, and traditional chili powder. In a large bowl (the one you will be mixing and serving in) whisk together the spices, garlic, 1 teaspoon salt and pepper, mustard and vinegar. Slowly stream in the oil, whisking to fully incorporate.

Toss the onions, celery, parsley and cilantro in the vinaigrette. Drain potatoes and return them to the pan for about 2 minutes. The heat from the pan evaporates a bit of the excess water in the potatoes. Add to bowl while still hot so the potatoes will absorb the flavorful vinaigrette. Toss in kale ribbons and adjust salt if necessary. Serve hot or room temperature.

Deconstructed BLT Salad with Creamy Avocado and Blue Cheese Crumbles

In August when the heirloom tomatoes are abundant this is such a welcomed salad, with peppery turkey bacon, crisp lettuce and creamy, buttery avocados and the sharp tang of my Yogurt and Blue Cheese . . . it doesn't even require dressing, just a sprinkle of black lava salt!
Serves 2

6 slices uncured, pepper turkey bacon
1 tablespoon olive oil
1 1/2 cups mixed heirloom tomatoes in small wedges
1 small avocado peeled, pitted and diced
1/2 teaspoon lemon juice
3 tablespoons Yogurt and Blue Cheese Crumbles
4 cups Romaine lettuce torn
Black lava salt

Fry turkey bacon in olive oil until very crisp. Drain on paper toweling to blot excess oil. Tear into bite sized pieces. Place cut tomatoes in a non-reactive bowl with avocado and sprinkle with lemon juice. Tear Romaine into bite sized pieces and add to bowl. Toss very lightly then add to serving platter. Top with bacon and blue cheese crumbles. Sprinkle with black salt and serve.

Vegan Deconstructed BLT Salad with Creamy Avocado and Goat Cheeze Crumbles

I created Temphe Bacon specifically for this dish. This salad is every bit as good as its cousin above, go ahead, give it a try, I promise you will not be disappointed.
Serves 2

Substitute 12 slices Crispy Tempeh Bacon and 1/4 cup crumbled Blue Cheeze and follow all other directions.

 # Wine Country Chicken Salad

This salad was inspired by a salad I used to buy at Huckleberry's Fresh Market in Spokane. I know the list of ingredients looks long, but it really is quick to assemble and totally worth the effort! A bit of pasta, a bit of chicken and a variety of flavor packed veggies. This salad is destined to become one of your favorites!
Serves 4

1 cup uncooked spelt or GF penne pasta
2 grilled chicken breast, sliced into 1/2 in strips
4 cups arugula
1/2 pound crimini mushrooms sliced
1 sundried tomato diced
1 roasted yellow pepper sliced into thin strips
1 cup cherry tomatoes halved
8 giant caperberries
½ cup Greek olives
½ cup artichoke hearts quartered
1 1/2 cups green beans
¼ cup roasted garlic
3 tablespoons grated Romano cheese
2 tablespoons toasted pine nuts
2 teaspoons coarsely chopped flat leaf parsley
2 teaspoons basil ribbons
1/4 cup Wine Country Vinaigrette

Boil pasta in heavily salted water just until tender. Drain and toss in a salad bowl with about 1/2 of the vinaigrette. Set aside. In a small sauté pan add 2 teaspoons of Herb Infused Olive Oil and sliced mushrooms. Sauté until soft and browned. Set aside to cool.

Place very young green beans, haricot vert are my favorite, in salted boiling water for about 2 minutes. Remove from water and place into a bowl of iced water. Layer the ingredients, top with remaining vinaigrette and toss. Serve and enjoy!

 # Wine Country Chick'n Salad

Repace grilled chicken breast with Tofu Chick'n (page 92-93) and Romano Cheese with Feta Cheeze Crumbles.

 Wine Country Vinaigrette

This is vinaigrette you will absolutely love! It has bright notes from the lemon, mellow, nutty roasted garlic adds another layer of flavor and the roasted walnut oil provides a rich finish. It is fabulous with the Wine Country Chicken Salad I created, but it is equally good with a side salad of your favorite greens.
Yield – 1/3 cup

3 tablespoons Lemon Infused White Balsamic Vinegar
1 tablespoon lemon juice
5 cloves roasted garlic
¼ teaspoon salt
¼ teaspoon pepper
1 tablespoon roasted walnut oil
¼ cup walnut oil
1 tablespoon Roasted Walnut and Basil Pesto

Place vinegar, lemon juice, garlic, salt, pepper and pesto in your VitaMix blender container and slowly blend until completely incorporated. Add the oils in a slow stream. Taste and adjust seasoning.

 # Roasted Chick'n Salad in Country Mustard Dressing with Broccoli, Cherry Tomatoes and Baby Spinach

This is a great vegan main dish salad that is so colorful you cannot resist taking a bite! The creamy and spicy mustard dressing makes the roasted tofu, tomatoes and broccoli sing. This is a terrific dish to serve at your next picnic or backyard party. It's flavor and nutrient packed with plenty of protein.
Serves 4

Tofu Chick'n Marinade

2 packages extra firm organic tofu, frozen, defrosted and water removed
1 teaspoon Celtic sea salt
1/2 teaspoon pepper
3 tablespoons Dijon mustard

1 tablespoon Veganaise
1 tablespoon Herb Infused Olive Oil
1 tablespoon nutritional yeast
1 teaspoon garlic granules

Country Mustard Dressing

3/4 cup Veganaise
3 tablespoons Dijon mustard
2 tablespoons whole grain mustard
2 tablespoons Tarragon Infused Vinegar
1 teaspoon Celtic sea salt
1 teaspoon freshly ground black pepper
1 tablespoon chopped fresh tarragon
1 teaspoon lemon zest
1 tablespoon lemon juice

Salad Veggies

1 1/2 cups cherry tomato halves
1 1/2 cups broccoli florettes
6 cups baby spinach
2 tablespoons roughly chopped Italian parsley

In a small bowl combine salt, pepper, mustard, Veganaise, nutritional yeast, garlic and oil. Cube tofu into bite sized pieces. Brush liberally with mustard mix and marinate for at least 2 hours or overnight. Place on an oiled baking sheet. Bake at 400 degrees for 12 – 15 minutes or until slightly crispy. Remove from oven, cool slightly then set aside.

In a separate bowl combine veganaise, mustard, vinegar, tarragon, lemon zest and juice, salt and pepper. Set aside.

Bring a pot of water to a brisk boil with 1 tablespoon Celtic sea salt and prepare an iced water bath. Blanch broccoli in boiling water until it is bright green. Plunge into iced water to shock the broccoli and stop the cooking.

Toss tomatoes, broccoli, tofu and dressing together until all ingredients are completely combined. Add spinach and toss until spinach is well distributed. Place on a serving platter and garnish with chopped Italian parsley.

Caramelized Leek and Roasted Potato Salad

Tender and caramelized roasted leeks and fingerling potatoes are the stars of this fresh approach to an old favorite. The addition of fresh greens, Roquefort cheese and fresh herbs let you know with every bite, this is no ordinary potato salad!
Serves 4

3 leeks
1 pound fingerling potatoes
2 tablespoons capers
1/4 cup mixed Greek olives
4 hardboiled eggs
2 hearts of Romaine
Salt and pepper
1/4 teaspoon garlic powder
1/4 cup Herbed Infused Oil, divided
1/2 teaspoon fresh thyme leaves
1/2 teaspoon chopped fresh rosemary leaves
1/2 teaspoon chopped fresh oregano leaves
1/4 cup Lemon, Herb and Roasted Leek Vinaigrette

Preheat oven to 400 degrees.

Halve leeks lengthwise and then cut across leeks in 2 inch pieces. Place in a colander and submerge in water. Allow the dirt to settle to the bottom of the water. Quickly lift out of the water. Repeat until water is clear. Drain well.

Scrub potatoes, remove any blemishes. Cut in half, lengthwise. Toss potatoes and leeks in herbs and oil. Spread on a baking sheet, sprinkle with salt, pepper and garlic powder. Bake on the bottom rack of the oven for about 30 minutes, turning over at least once to be certain both sides are golden and sugars have caramelized. Remove from oven, cool for about 5 minutes then toss in bowl with capers, olives, and dressing. The veggies will immediately soak up the flavors.

Meanwhile, boil eggs, cool, peel and slice into lengthwise quarters.

Tear lettuce into bite sized pieces and pile on a serving platter. Place eggs around edges and top with veggies. Sprinkle with Roquefort and serve.

Creamy Lemon, Herb and Roasted Leek Vinaigrette

I created this dressing for my Caramelized Leek and Roasted Potato Salad, but it is a great complement to any combo of greens!
Yield – 2/3 cup

3 tablespoons Herb Infused Olive Oil
2 teaspoons Herb Infused White Wine Vinegar
2 tablespoons freshly squeezed lemon juice
1 tablespoon Crème Cheese Substitute
½ teaspoon Dijon mustard
¼ teaspoon each, rosemary, thyme and oregano
2 inch piece caramelized leek
1 small pinch stevia or 1/2 teaspoon honey
¼ teaspoon Celtic sea salt
¼ teaspoon freshly ground black pepper

In a VitaMix place leek, stevia, herbs, mustard, crème cheese, lemon juice and vinegar. Slowly drizzle in oil, then salt and pepper. Taste and adjust seasoning.

Lemon, Caper and Dill Marinade and Sauce

This is a perfectly tart, salty and herb infused marinade that takes just seconds to prepare. The great thing about it is that it does double duty. Spread some on your fish, chicken or tofu to marinate and then use the remainder in the sauté pan. It will thicken slightly and become a very silky sauce to spoon over your finished product! I developed it specifically for my Mock Halibut, and found that it was so easy and delicious it has become one of my "go to" preparations for halibut and salmon in my kitchen.
Yield – 3/4 cup

2 tablespoons Lemon Infused Olive Oil
2 large cloves garlic minced
1 tablespoon finely chopped fresh dill
2 teaspoons lemon zest
2 tablespoons lemon juice

¼ teaspoon Dijon mustard
½ teaspoon drained and rinsed capers
1 large pinch Celtic sea salt and freshly ground pepper

Whisk together. Refrigerated, it will keep up to 3 days in a tightly sealed glass jar. Should any of the lemon juice separate out, simply shake vigorously.

Country Style Egg Salad in Butter Lettuce Cups

Your next picnic, hike or backyard get together is a great excuse to make egg salad. While this recipe is a bit lower in fat, the addition of mustard and crunchy veggies make it taste even better than of the traditional dish. Making your own mayo allows you to use healthy sources of essential fatty acids and tons of flavor. If you like you can serve it on your favorite bread or roll, burrito style in the lettuce leaves.
Serves 4 - 6

1/3 cup Basic Blender Mayo
2 teaspoons chopped fresh dill plus sprigs for garnish
1/2 teaspoon celery seeds
1 tablespoon Dilled Vinegar
1 tablespoon yellow mustard
1 tablespoon Dijon mustard
1/4 teaspoon Celtic sea salt
1/4 teaspoon freshly ground black pepper
1/4 cup finely sliced green onion
1/2 cup finely chopped celery
1/3 cup finely chopped red bell pepper
6 eggs
4 butter lettuce leaves

Place eggs in a pot large enough so the eggs are not too crowded. Cover with cold pH 9.5 ionized water or filtered water with 1 teaspoon white vinegar. Bring to a boil over medium heat, cover, turn off heat and leave on burner for 10 minutes. Place eggs in an ice water bath, peel and chop. Mix with chopped onion, celery and red pepper.

Meanwhile, mix mayo, dill, vinegar, mustards, celery seeds, salt and pepper. Taste and adjust seasonings if necessary. Pour over eggs and veggies, then stir to blend. Let it sit for a few minutes so flavors can meld a bit, taste and adjust seasonings if necessary.

To serve place lettuce leaves (choose leaves from nearer the center of the head, they tend to be shaped more like cups) on a serving tray and scoop or spoon egg salad into cups. Garnish with a sprinkle of paprika and a dill sprig.

Lemon and Dill Vinaigrette

This dressing was designed specifically for my version of an old French classic, Salade Niçoise . It is equally flavored with the bright flavors of lemon and dill since both complement the flavors of veggies, eggs and fish. So feel free to use it any time!
Yield – ½ cup

3 tablespoons lemon juice
1 teaspoon lemon zest
2 tablespoons white wine vinegar
1 tablespoon finely chopped fresh dill
1 teaspoon finely minced garlic
1 tablespoon finely minced shallot
1 teaspoon Italian Seasoning paste
¼ cup Lemon Infused Olive Oil
½ teaspoon agave nectar or a small pinch of stevia
¼ teaspoon salt and pepper

I prefer to use an immersion blender for this vinaigrette, but you can use any style of blender you choose. Here are a couple of other tips, if you have not yet made Lemon Infused Olive Oil, simply use regular extra virgin olive oil and increase the lemon zest to 2 teaspoons. I generally always keep Italian Seasoning Paste (it's my secret flavor booster) in my refrigerator, but if you do not have it you can substitute 1 teaspoon of dried Italian seasoning herbs or a teaspoon of basil pesto if you're in a pinch.

Put everything in your blender container and blend for about 30 seconds. Taste, adjust the salt, pepper and agave to your taste. It should be very tart but not too acidic.

⭐ OMG! Updated Salade Niçoise

The classic French version of this wonderful salad uses tuna, but given the fact that tuna is no longer a healthy seafood choice, I've given it a bit of an update . . . halibut. It's mild in flavor and high in Omega 3 fatty acids, making it the perfect heart healthy choice! Each component is delicious on its own, but when tied together with a tart, fresh, lemony dressing, the sum is greater than the total of its individual parts!
Serves 4

1 pound very small red or fingerling potatoes
2 garlic cloves
8 ounces haricot vert or small green beans
4 hardboiled eggs
4 4 ounce pieces Herbed Halibut in Parchment Paper
12 giant caperberries
1/2 cup Greek or kalamata olives
1 pint cherry tomatoes
12 leaves red butter lettuce
Lemon and Dill Vinaigrette

Boil potatoes in heavily salted water with 1 garlic clove. When tender drain and return to hot pan for 5 minutes to evaporate any excess water. Pour about 1.3 of the vinaigrette over the hot potatoes. Cool to room temperature.

In the meantime, fill a medium sized stock pot filled with water to a boil. Add 1 tablespoon salt and the green beans. Cook about 3-4 minutes or until beans are bright green. Remove beans from the water and immediately plunge into a bowl of iced water to stop the cooking. Drain thoroughly.

Arrange lettuce leaves on a large serving tray. Refer to the photo and mound ingredients around the platter, topping it with caperberries. Drizzle remaining vinaigrette on salad.

Vegetarian Salade Niçoise

Replace halibut with Mock Halibut and enjoy!

Sonoma Grilled Chicken Salad

Grilled chicken breasts make a huge difference in this traditional salad! I prefer the crunch of hearts of romaine, but you can also serve over tender butter lettuce leaves that hold the chicken salad as though they were little cups.
Serves 4

6 cups sliced romaine hearts or butter lettuce
1 1/2 cups cubed grilled chicken breast
1 cup diced granny smith or gala apple
1 cup thinly sliced celery
1 cup grapes, halved
1/4 cup finely diced red onion
1/4 cup toasted walnuts, rough chopped
1/4 cup cubed goat's milk gouda

3 tablespoons Lemonnaise
1 teaspoon Dijon mustard
2 tablespoons flat leaf Italian Parsley
1 teaspoon lemon zest
1 tablespoon lemon juice
2 tablespoons apple juice
Salt and pepper to taste

In a small bowl whisk Lemonaise, mustard, roughly
chopped parsley, lemon juice and zest, apple juice, salt and pepper until smooth and creamy.

In a large bowl gently toss the chicken, apple, celery, grapes, onions, walnuts and cheese. Add dressing and turn to coat.

To serve place lettuce on plate and divide chicken salad among plates. Garnish with flat leaf Italian parsley and serve.

Saffron Rice Salad

This is a terrific salad that can stand alone as a main dish, or as a side salad. Inspired by the flavors of the Kashmiri region of the Near East, the vibrant colors, the complex textures and combination of sweet, tangy and spicy flavors make this a memorable salad. It holds well for several hours so it's a great choice for a buffet menu item. Serve it chilled or room temperature. To add additional protein to this dish, try Coconut Tofu or Coconut Chicken.

Yield - 4 main course or 8 salad course servings

4 cups saffron rice, chilled
1 1/2 cups Fresh Tropical Fruit Chutney
3 Tablespoons pistachio oil
1/3 cup pineapple juice
1/4 cup chiffonade of mint leaves
1 teaspoon lime zest
1/3 cup lime juice
6 cups baby spinach leaves
1/4 cup Kashmiri Almonds
1/4 cup lightly toasted pistachios
1/4 cup Curried Cashews
2 ounces Black Pepper and Honey Yogurt Cheese or Honeyed Goat Cheeze Crumbles

Garnish:

Chunks of pineapple, papaya and mango skewered and grilled (grilling optional)
Cilantro and mint leaves

Mix chutney, oil, lime zest and fruit juices together to create a dressing for the salad.

Toss chilled rice, spinach and crumbled cheese together. Carefully mix in chutney. Sprinkle nuts over the salad, if this is going to be served buffet style or made ahead, sprinkle the nuts on just before your guests arrive to keep them crunchy.

To prepare the grilled fruit skewers, cut fruit into similarly sized pieces, brush with either coconut or pistachio oil and place on a grill over low heat for about 1 minute per side.

Garnish with fruit skewer, mint and cilantro leaves.

Quinoa Tabouli Salad

I really love Mediterranean foods and missed wheat laden tabouli, so when I decided to try quinoa as a replacement for the bulgur I never guessed it would taste even better! While white quinoa is good in this recipe, red quinoa has a slightly chewier texture that's much more like bulgur. Taking time to soak and then toast the quinoa before cooking makes it taste even better.

Yield – 6 servings

1 cup red quinoa
1 1/4 cups water
1/8 teaspoon Celtic sea salt

1 1/2 cups cherry tomatoes halved
1 1/2 cups cucumber sliced
3 cloves roasted garlic diced
1/2 cup parsley
1/4 cup mint
1/4 cup diced red onion

1/3 cup lemon juice
2 teaspoons tahini
3 tablespoons Garlic Infused Olive Oil
1/2 teaspoon Bruschetta Spice Blend
1/2 teaspoon Celtic sea salt

Rinse quinoa well, then soak in pH 9.5 ionized water for 20 minutes. Rinse and drain well. Toast quinoa over medium heat until it begins to smell fragrant. Add salt and water, cover and bring to a boil for 5 minutes. Turn the heat off and leave on burner and the quinoa will continue to steam for 20 minutes. Fluff with a fork. Pour on half the dressing while quinoa is still hot so it will absorb the flavors.

To make the dressing whisk together lemon juice, tahini, oil and spices until completely emulsified.

While quinoa is cooling, prep the herbs and veggies, sprinkle with salt and set aside 5 minutes before combining with quinoa and remaining dressing. Traditionally tabouli is served in Romaine leaves and topped with a little fresh mint as a garnish. Alternatively you can serve in Belgian endive leaves to make little "boats" then pass as finger food.

Country Style Dill and Mustard Potato Salad

This version is a bit lighter and healthier version of my Mom's potato salad. Every bite is a reminder of my childhood! Whether you are having a picnic or a grilling party, this one is always a crowd pleaser. Definitely better day 2 so make plenty!

Serves 6-8

1 ¼ pounds red potatoes diced (about 4 cups)
1 tablespoon Celtic sea salt
¼ teaspoon garlic powder
 6 eggs very coarsely chopped
1 tablespoon chopped fresh dill
¼ cup dill pickle relish, do not drain
2/3 cup diced sweet onions like Walla Walla or Vidalia
1 cup diced celery
¼ teaspoon Celtic sea salt
¼ teaspoon freshly ground black pepper

For dressing blend the following together:
1 tablespoon yellow mustard
3 tablespoons Basic Blender Mayonnaise
1 tablespoon apple cider vinegar
½ teaspoon celery seeds
1 teaspoon chopped fresh dill
Pinch stevia or 1 teaspoon agave
2 tablespoons Crème Cheese Substitute
Celtic sea salt and freshly ground pepper to taste
1 dash cayenne pepper

Boil potatoes in heavily salted water and garlic until fork tender. Drain and return to the pan for about 5 minutes to dry the potatoes. While warm dice potatoes, add onions, and about half of the dressing. Refrigerate until cool.

Meanwhile, place eggs in a pot, cover with water and bring to a boil over medium high heat. Turn the heat off, cover and eggs will continue cooking in the hot water. Allow to sit about 8 minutes. Drain, place in an ice water bath, peel and coarsely chop. Set aside.

To the potato mixture add remaining dressing, dill, relish and salt and pepper. Stir to thoroughly blend. Taste and adjust seasonings. Now add eggs and carefully incorporate.

Refrigerate at least 2 hours to overnight to allow flavors to meld.

Vegan Country Style Dill and Mustard Potato Salad with Crispy Tempeh Bac'n

With only minor changes, this vegan version of my Mom's potato salad is delicious. With the addition of crispy bits of Tempeh Bacaon even your egg loving friends will likely not notice, so serve it up at your next picnic or a grilling party, for rave reviews! Definitely better day 2 so make plenty!
Serves 6-8

Make these simple changes to the salad portion of the previous recipe:
Delete eggs
6 slices Tempeh Bacon cooked until very crispy and crumble into small pieces
Increase the quantity to 2 ¼ lbs baby red potatoes

Make these changes to the dressing portion of the previous recipe:
Substitute Veganaise for Basic Blender Mayonnaise
Increase apple cider vinegar to 1 1/2 tablespoons
Add 1 teaspoon lemon juice
Increase agave to 1 1/2 teaspoons
Substitute Sour Supreme for Creme Cheese Substitute

Halve baby red potatoes and cook according to directions. These pretty potatoes become the star of the salad and using slightly bigger pieces makes the salad seem more substantial.

Since Veganaise is more mild in flavor, adding a little lemon juice and increasing the vinegar will give it the same punch as the blender mayo.

Follow all remaining instructions. Add bacon pieces just before serving to keep them crispy.

Pear and Fennel Salad with Watercress and Goat Cheese

As summer begins to move into fall, new fruit and veggie selections begin to appear. Two of the things that begin to appear at my local farmers' market I adore are ripe pears and crunchy, anise flavored, fresh fennel, so I decided to pair them with some sweet and spicy walnuts, peppery watercress, a tangy vinaigrette and some creamy goat cheese . . . just recording this recipe makes me want another salad! Add on some warm No Knead Ciabatta to serve 2 as a main course or serve 4 as a salad course. It is a great pairing with Lemon Roasted Chicken or Stuffed and Roasted Portobello Mushrooms.

1 large bartlett, bosc or d'anjou pear
1 ½ cups thinly sliced fennel bulb
1/3 cup Sweet and Savory Italian Style Walnuts
1 bunch watercress
¼ cup Goat Cheeze crumbles or fresh goat cheese slices

Wash and spin or pat dry watercress, remove any longish stems. Place in a large bowl. Using a mandolin shave fennel bulb or slice as thinly aspossible with a sharp knife, then toss in bowl. Coarsely chop fennel fronds and set aside.

Roughly chop walnuts and set aside.

Halve pear and remove core with a small melon baller or spoon. Turn cut side down and slice pears into ¼ inch slices. Keeping them in tact until ready to dress to preserve color.   Place in bowl.

Gently toss watercress, pears and fennel with dressing. Sprinkle with fennel fronds, walnuts and cheese.

Blueberry Mojito Salad

This salad is so refreshing, beautiful to look, delicious so nutrient dense it made it on my OMG! All-Star list! the combination of sweet-tart blueberries, tender baby spinach, creamy cheese and the exotic flavors of the Mojito Vinaigrette make each bite a flavor sensation. I predict it is destined to be one of your favorite quick salads. When fresh blueberries are not available, try strawberries, raspberries or dried cranberries for a new twist. (Pictured on page 78.)
Yield - 2 large or 4 side salads

4 cups baby spinach
1/2 cup fresh blueberries
1 ounce goat's milk gouda cheese or Goat Cheeze Crumbles
1 tablespoon coarse lemon zest
3 tablespoons Mojito Vinaigrette

Break cheese into chunks with a fork.

In a large bowl toss spinach and blueberries until vinaigrette is well distributed. Divide among plates and sprinkle with lemon zest, cheese and a sprig of mint.

Mojito Vinaigrette

This tangy and minty, citrus based dressing is reminiscent of one of my favorite cocktails . . . There are only a few ingredietns yet the flavor is complex and so delicious! I generally prefer my dressings made fresh just before serving, but this one holds up for a few days!
Yeild - 1/2 cup

2 tablespoons freshly squeezed lime juice
2 tablespoons freshly squeezed lemon juice
3 tablespoons Lemon Infused Olive Oil
1 teaspoon lime zest
1 teaspoon agave nectar or 1/8 teaspoon stevia
1 tablespoon finely chopped mint leaves
1/8 teaspoon each sea salt and black teaspoon pepper

This dressing is best when blended to fully incorporate the mint leaves with the citrus juices and oil. Tightly cap, refrigerate and store up to 4 days.

Soups, Stocks and Broths

I love soup! Maybe it's because I've lived most of my life in places where there are four distinct seasons and soup is just so hearty and satisfying on a chilly day. From the aroma wafting through the house to the warmth it provides to any meal . . . soup is undeniably perfect in every way . . . even chilled soups in the summer are the perfect solution to the long, hot, dog days of August!

Of course when you consider nutrition, a single bowl of soup can really pack in the veggies and the fiber! When my kids were small they were not vegetable enthusiasts, so soup was one way to hide all the veggies in a yummy broth and voilè I had them eating things they would ordinarily never touch!

And let's not forget the efficiency of soup - it's a perfect one pot meal. Plus you can make a big pot of soup and it will last for a couple of days, or better yet, freeze some in serving size portions for a quick "go to" meal on a busy day . . . simply team with a simple salad for a complete meal that is every bit as delicious as it is nutritious!

The thing about soup is that the stock is the single most important component in every soup. You will find recipes for homemade, long simmering stock as well as a quick and easy solution that is ready In less than 2 minutes!

The recipes in this section include my favorite chilled soups, my famous chilies and garden veggie varities. When it comes to entertaining these are great options that will free you from the kitchen and provide your friends and family with something they will be talking about for years!

So follow my lead and make big batches to share with friends and neighbors, and take advantage of the freezer so that at the end of a busy day there will always be a bowl of soup avaialble . . . I predict that you will soon be saying . . . "I love soup!"

 Vegetable Stock

This is my favorite long simmering veggie stock. It is so rich and flavorful that I love to just sip a cup on a cold afternoon for a super nutritious pick-me-up. By keeping the temperature just below the boiling point, it retains nearly all of the vitamins and minerals from the veggies as well as all of the flavor! When making stock it is very important to use as many organic veggies as possible. Since this one takes some time to cook, simply put it on the stove at bedtime and when you get up in the morning it is finished!

Yield - 1 gallon

6 large carrots cut into 3 inch pieces
6 celery ribs cut into 3 inch pieces
2 baking potatoes quartered
3 yellow or white onions quartered
2 heads garlic cut in half
2 turnips cut in half
2 parsnips cut into 3 inch pieces
1 head green cabbage cut into quarters
2 cups green beans
4 golden beets cut in half (red beets make the broth red)
1/2 cup parsley (this is a great place to use the stems)
4 sprigs each rosemary, sage and oregano
10 thyme sprigs
1 tablespoon whole peppercorns and Tuscan Salt Blend
3 tablespoons nutritional yeast

Place all veggies and herbs in a 2 gallon stock pot, cover with pH 9.5 ionized water. Cover and cook over very low heat 10 hours. Strain and divide among storage containers. Use as the base for your favorite soups!

Kitchen Tip: As you prepare veggies, save the trimmings for stock. Even onion and garlic skins have loads of flavor. Simply drop them in a zipper bag and pop them in the freezer. In no time you will have plenty to make stock. In addition to quart jars, try freezing stock in ice cube trays. It's both flavorful and nutrient dense so adding just a few tablespoons can boost the nutritional content of your favorite dishes!

Flavorful Quick Veggie Stock

The most important component in any soup is the stock. If you start with a bland and watery stock your dish will suffer from the same taste. Of course homemade stock is the very best but if you don't have the time to make it or the space to freeze it, don't worry. This version starts with a boxed stock and a few more ingredients to balance and intensify the flavors. It takes only a minute to complete it.
Yield – 2 quarts

2 quart boxes Pacific Vegetable Stock
1 cup organic Mushroom Broth
1/4 cup Seitenbacher or Oregon brand vegetable powder
1 cup dry white wine

Combine all ingredients in a stock pot and bring to a simmer. Freeze in ice cube trays and just pop them into any recipe for a pop of flavor!

Fish Stock

A simple, quick variation to your favorite Vegetable Stock for seafood soups, stews. This is a great way to use otherwise unusable portions of fish. In fact, most fish departments actually give away fish bones and they are perfect for making stock. I freeze some in ice cube trays for just a hint of the sea anytime I want it.
Yield – 3 quarts

2 quarts Vegetable Stock
1 cup fennel tops and fronds
2 quarts pH 9.5 ionized water
2 pounds fish bones or scraps

Place all ingredients in a large stock pot, bring to a gentle boil, reduce heat and simmer until flavorful. Strain and transfer to glass jars for storage.

Chilled Asparagus Soup 2 Ways

There are few things that are more refreshing and satisfying than this soup. Depending on your personal tastes and the level of effort you are willing to exert, there are 2 options for serving this delicious soup. The first is simple, beautiful and light. The second is more intricate and includes a bit of salmon – the quintessential partner to asparagus and dill . . . No matter which you choose, this soup is an excellent choice for a simple patio setting or an elegant brunch! (Photo page 78)
Serves 6-8

1 tablespoon olive oil
3 cups sliced leeks, white and light green parts only
1 cup sliced celery
1 tablespoon chopped garlic
2 lbs asparagus
2 baking potatoes, diced
2 quarts Flavorful Vegetable Stock
2 teaspoons vegetable bouillon
2 teaspoons fresh dill, chopped
1 + teaspoons Celtic sea salt and white pepper
4 tablespoons Crème Fraîche Substitute

Since this is a blended soup it isn't necessary to chop the vegetables too finely or peel the potatoes if you are using a powerful blender like a VitaMix; if you are using an immersion blender smaller pieces and peeled potatoes are a must. In a large, heavy bottomed 4 quart saucepan over medium heat, sweat the onions, celery, garlic and vegetable bouillon in olive oil until onions are translucent. Add diced potatoes. Stir to coat with oil and to season. Add 2 tablespoons vegetable stock, cover and allow the potatoes to steam and soften a bit, about 5 minutes. Be certain to stir occasionally to ensure garlic does not begin to brown.

Meanwhile, prepare asparagus by snapping off any woody bottoms (if you make fresh vegetable juice reserve for later use, otherwise toss them in your compost bin). Remove the tips from the asparagus and set aside. Cut the stems into 1-inch lengths and add them to the pot. Add the remaining stock, dill and cut asparagus stems. Bring to a simmer for 15-20 minutes but do not boil. When potatoes are fork tender remove from heat. Cool slightly and blend until soup is silky smooth. Taste and adjust seasonings. Strain through a sieve or mesh strainer to remove any fibers. Cover and refrigerate until cold – about 90 minutes and up to 24 hours.

This soup is equally delicious hot or warm as well as chilled. Either way garnish with one of the following options.

Garnish

While your soup is simmering, bring a small pot of well salted water to a boil over high heat.   Blanch the asparagus tips – drop in boiling water for 2 to 3 minutes, then immediately plunge into an ice water bath. Remove with a slotted spoon, lay them out on a kitchen towel, pat dry and reserve for the garnish.

To serve, ladle soup into chilled bowls, place a dollop of Crème Fraîche Substitute in the center of the bowl. With the blade of a knife, create a swirl pattern, top with a small stack of asparagus tips. Serve immediately.

Alternate Serving Suggestion:

You will need the following additional ingredients:
1 large avocado, peeled and pitted
1 teaspoon lemon juice
1 pinch of salt, white and cayenne pepper
1 tablespoon finely minced shallot
8 tablespoons baked salmon with skin removed and broken into small flakes
1/3 cup Crème Fraîche Substitute,
1 tablespoon chopped dill and a pinch of salt and white pepper

In a small bowl mash avocado with lemon juice, salt, peppers and shallot. In a separate bowl carefully fold 2 tablespoons Creme Fraiche Substute, dill, salt and pepper into flaked salmon.

In the center of each chilled bowl, place a tall cylindrical biscuit or cookie cutter, which you have lightly sprayed with olive oil. Begin building a layered tower in each bowl starting with 1 tablespoon of the avocado mash to anchor it to the bowl. Top the avocado with a tablespoon of the flaked salmon mixture and press down lightly with the back of a spoon to compact the layers slightly, top the salmon with a thin layer of Crème Fraîche Substitute, then asparagus tips, lightly compact once again. Repeat, ending with asparagus tips. Top your asparagus tips with a small dot of Crème Fraîche Substitute and a small sprig of dill for added flare. Now you have created what pantry chefs call a timbale. Be sure you have created enough height so that your last 2 layers will stand above your soup.

Ladle the soup into the bowl until the desired depth is achieved then carefully remove the cookie cutter. (At this point you will likely want to hold your breath and say a word of thanks to the person who invented a sprayer for olive oil.) Stand back and admire, then serve immediately.

Icy-Hot Watermelon Gazpacho

This chilled soup is a contradiction in tastes and textures. It is hot and cool, creamy and crunchy, spicy and tangy . . . and best of all this delicious soup packs a nutritional punch. It contains high levels of lycopene, capsaicin, vitamin C and heart healthy fats, plus all the minerals necessary to balance your electrolytes! What a delicious and refreshing way to bring balance to your body on a hot summer's day . . .
Yield – 4 8 oz servings

Soup Base
2 ½ cups watermelon juice
¼ in square piece of habanero pepper
3 tablespoons cilantro leaves
Juice and zest of 1 lime
¼ tsp Celtic sea salt

This makes a very spicy base despite the small amount of Habanero. If you would like a milder version substitute 1-2 tablespoons seeded jalapeno pepper.

½ cup diced cucumber
2 tablespoons each diced red, yellow and orange bell pepper
3 tablespoons diced red onion 1 tablespoon
1 tablespoon thinly sliced green onion
½ teaspoon minced garlic
3 tablespoons thinly sliced celery
Juice of 1 lime
1 medium avocado diced (reserve half)
2 cups watermelon diced in 1/2 inch pieces (reserve half)
¼ cup yogurt – use your favorite brand of coconut, goat or sheep's milk yogurt
Cilantro sprigs
Lime sliced quartered

Chill base in freezer until ice crystals are beginning to form. Run a fork through as if you were making granita and allow a second layer of crystals to form. Meanwhile prepare all remaining ingredients and place in the freezer for about 20 minutes so everything is cold. Toss avocado in lime juice.

Combine everything except garnish and ladle into small bowls. Add a small dollop of yogurt then garnish with a few pieces of watermelon and avocado, a small sprig of cilantro and a piece of lime.

Chilled Melon Soup

This soup is light, refreshing and a perfect beginning to any summer meal. So delicious that you   will find yourself
making this one over and over again during the hot summer days and so beautiful it makes a terrific   addition to a fancy
brunch.
Serves 4

1 large honeydew melon, peeled, seeded and chopped
1/2 cantaloupe scooped into balls
2 teaspoons lemon juice
1/4 cup mint leaves + 4 mint sprigs
1 pinch Celtic sea salt
8 ounces goat, sheep's milk or coconut yogurt

In a VitaMix or other powerful blender puree honeydew, lemon juice, mint, salt and 3/4 cup yogurt until smooth. Chill up to
12 hours.

Divide cantaloupe balls between bowls ladle honeydew puree over melon balls. Add 1 tablespoon yogurt to each bowl
and swirl. Garnish with a sprig of mint and serve.

Chilled Cucumber Soup with White Truffle Oil

This is a wonderfully light, yet satisfying chilled soup. It's so beautiful and delicate yet versatile. Serve with a crisp salad it can be the star of the meal for a light lunch or simply a refreshing start to a sumptuous feast . . .
Yield – 2 servings

2 pounds English (seedless) cucumbers
3 cups yellow tomatoes roughly chopped plus ¼ cup finely chopped
1 medium yellow bell pepper roughly chopped
1/3 cup chopped white onion
2 tablespoons white balsamic or Champaign vinegar
4 teaspoons finely chopped fresh dill
1 tablespoon finely chopped Italian flat leaf parsley
1 tablespoon minced garlic
Celtic sea salt and white pepper to taste
2 teaspoons white truffle oil
Italian flat leaf parsley leaves
Dill fronds
3 tablespoons Sour Creme Substitute

Roughly chop cucumbers, reserving half of a cucumber for garnish. Combine the cucumber and tomatoes in a VitaMix or other powerful blender. Add the bell pepper, onion, vinegar, 1 teaspoon each dill and parsley, 1 clove garlic and the sugar; puree until smooth. Pass through a fine mesh strainer into a bowl, pressing with the back of a spoon to extract as much liquid as possible. Season with approximately 1 teaspoon of salt and ½ teaspoon of white pepper, taste and adjust seasoning to suite your preference. Refrigerate until chilled, about 2 hours or overnight.

Meanwhile prepare the garnish. Place ½ cup of your favorite yogurt in a coffee filter lined strainer over a bowl and drain. Slice remaining cucumber into matchstick pieces about 2 ½ inches long. Finely chop ¼ cup yellow tomatoes, tear a few parsley leaves and dill fronds from stems.

Ladle soup into individual chilled bowls. Garnish with a dollop of yogurt, a few finely chopped yellow tomatoes, matchstick pieces of cucumber set at an angle, flat leaf parsley leaves, dill fronds, then drizzle with white truffle oil. Serve immediately.

 # Garden Veggie Soup

If you are fortunate enough to have your own garden or simply have access to a great organic farmers' market, you know that there are weeks when the fresh produce seems to explode! This yummy veggie soup is a fantastic way to capture the essence of all of those veggies in one dish. Make extra to freeze so you can experience that flavor through the cold months of winter. This version contains a wide variety of veggies, so feel free to customize it to fit what's available.
Yield – 2 gallons

1 tablespoon Herb Infused Olive Oil
3 cups diced yellow onions (1 large)
2 tablespoons finely minced garlic (4 cloves)
1 1/2 cups sliced carrots (2 large)
1 1/2 cups zucchini (1 medium)
1 1/2 cups yellow squash (1 medium)
1 cup red pepper diced
1 cup green beans
1 cup yellow wax beans
2 cups potatoes (1 large)
1 1/2 cups celery (2 ribs)
2 cups cabbage
4 cups kale
2 cups diced tomatoes
3 sprigs thyme, rosemary, oregano and sage
1 teaspoon coarse black pepper
1/4 teaspoon red pepper flakes
1/4 cup nutritional yeast
2 quarts water
2 quarts Vegetable Stock

To a large stock pot over medium heat add oil, onions, garlic and celery. Sweat until tender, stirring occasionally. Add potatoes and carrots and continue cooking about 3 minutes. Tie herbs with kitchen twine and drop into pot. Add remaining vegetables, stock, water, nutritional yeast, red and black pepper. Cover and simmer about 1 hour. Adjust seasonings and serve.

French Lentil Soup with Wilted Spinach

This soup is one of my all-time favorite soups. Its flavors are deceptively complex and rich while using so few ingredients and so little cooking time. Serve it with some crusty bread for a complete meal.
Serves 6

1 1/2 cups French lentils
1 cup water
3 1/2 cups Quick and Flavorful Veggie Stock
1 1/2 cups diced yellow onion
1 tablespoon finely minced garlic
1 tablespoon ground cumin
1 can Thai Kitchen organic coconut milk
3 tablespoons San-J GF low sodium tamari
6 cups packed baby spinach

Rinse then soak lentils in water about 10 minutes. Drain well and place in a stockpot with water. Bring to a boil over medium heat for about 10 minutes.

Add Veggie Stock, onion, garlic, cumin, coconut milk and tamari, cover and simmer until lentils are tender, 30-40 minutes.

To serve place spinach in the bottom of each soup plate or bowl. Ladle tender lentils and coconut broth over the spinach. Garnish with a spoonful of unsweetened Coconut Crème.

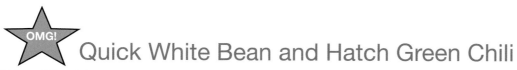

Quick White Bean and Hatch Green Chili

When I lived in Albuquerque September meant one thing – Hatch green chiles roasting over open flames . . . the aroma was almost intoxicating! They are available in 2 varieties, mild and hot, so choose the style that you prefer for this super fast, thick, white bean chili with smoky Hatch chiles. If you can't find them fresh or roasted in your produce isle, they are available canned in the international foods isle. This is sure to be one of your favorite quick soups!
Serves 6-8

2 cans chick peas
2 cans cannelini beans
2 cans white navy beans
2 1/2 cups fire roasted Hatch green chilies
2 cups diced onions
2 tablespoons finely minced garlic
1 tablespoon olive oil
1 tablespoon cumin
1/4 teaspoon red pepper flakes
2 tablespoons nutritional yeast
1 teaspoon Better Than Bouillon
1 cup water

In a 3 quart stock pot, over medium heat sweat onions and garlic until onions are translucent. Add spices, green chilis, cannelini and navy beans.

Drain chick peas, puree with water, bouillon and nutritional yeast until smooth, stir in, heat thoroughly and ladle into warm bowls. It could not be faster!

Garnish with a spoonful of diced chilies and a sprig of cilantro or to add another layer of nutrition, garnish with steamed kale ribbons, roasted red peppers and steamed carrots.

Texas Style Chicken and Black Bean Chili

Texans take their chili seriously, and for good reason . . . it's seriously good! Thick, spicy and very hearty! This is a pretty traditional version using ground chicken, with a few hidden veggies that elevates chili to a wholly nutritious meal. I predict that when your neighbors smell it they will all be hoping for an invitation to dinner. This one makes enough for a crowd, so invite some friends over for a spectacular chili feast. Add some grated goat cheddar, Sour Crème Substitute, snipped chives and a few tortilla chips plus a salad and some Jalapeno Cornbread for a complete meal.
Yield – 1 gallon

1 tablespoon olive oil
4 cups diced onions, about 2 large
3 tablespoons finely minced garlic
1 1/2 pounds ground chicken or turkey
2 cups diced red pepper
1/2 cup grated celery
1 cup finely grated carrot
1 cup finely grated zucchini
2 cups finely chopped kale
28 ounce can Muir Glen crushed fire roasted tomatoes
2 14 ounce cans Muir Glen diced tomatoes with green chiles
3 15 ounce cans organic black beans
1/4 cup chopped cilantro
3 tablespoons chili powder
5 teaspoons cumin powder
1/2 teaspoon cayenne pepper
1 teaspoon red pepper flakes
1 teaspoon Mexican oregano
1 teaspoon salt

In a 4 quart stock pot, over medium heat, sweat onions and garlic in oil. Add ground chicken and cook until browned, add red peppers, celery, carrot, zucchini and kale. Stir to combine, cover and heat thoroughly before adding tomatoes and beans. Add spices and salt, cover and simmer over very low heat for at least 3 hours – the longer you simmer the better it gets.

Texas Style Veggie Chili

When it comes to chili, even vegetarians in Texas take their chili seriously, so it has to be as seriously good as any other Texas chili to earn the right to be dubbed a true Texas chili! This version uses soy chorizo to add that extra spicy goodness, plus a few hidden veggies to make a totally satisfying, thick, hearty chili that's a wholly nutritious meal. I predict that when your neighbors smell it they will all be hoping for an invitation to dinner and they will never know it's vegetarian unless you tell them! This recipe makes enough for a crowd, so invite some friends over for a spectacular chili feast. Add a salad and some cornbread for a complete meal.

Yield – 1 gallon

1 tablespoon olive oil
4 cups diced onions, about 2 large
3 tablespoons finely minced garlic
12 ounces soy chorizo
2 cups diced red pepper
1/2 cup grated celery
1 cup finely grated carrot
1 cup finely grated zucchini
2 cups finely chopped kale
28 ounce can crushed fire roasted tomatoes
14 ounce can diced tomatoes with green chiles
15 ounce can organic black beans
15 ounce can organic kidney beans
15 ounce can organic chili beans
1/4 cup chopped cilantro
3 tablespoons chili powder
1 tablespoon cumin powder
1/2 teaspoon cayenne pepper
1 teaspoon red pepper flakes
1 teaspoon Mexican oregano
1 teaspoon salt

In a 6 quart stock pot, over medium heat, sweat onions and garlic in oil. Add chorizo and thoroughly incorporate, add red peppers, celery, carrot, zucchini and kale. Stir to combine, cover and heat through before adding tomatoes and beans. Add spices and salt, cover and simmer over very low heat for at least 3 hours – the longer you simmer the better it gets.

VEGGIES AND SIDES

Vegetables are not just side dishes, they are the main ingredients that cover a plate of beautiful food. From roasted beets and squashes to steamed and jewel studded greens, from simple preparations to beautiful main dishes, the recipes in this section are no ordinary side dishes, they can truly be the stars of the meal!

From the time I was a really little girl I have loved vegetables! Not just the "normal" offerings that accompanied meals in the 1950's and 60's, but all of the unusual ones as well. I was that little girl who loved lima beans, Brussels sprouts and beets as much as fresh corn on the cob, tiny baby green beans and pencil thin asparagus . . . and of course tomatoes!

Now my children were the polar opposite – all 3 were not so enamored by them as children. In fact when my daughter Angela was in the 8th grade the big BSE cattle news broke across the world. She commented by saying, "it's enough to make me want to become a vegetarian, too bad I only like carrots . . . I guess I'll have to become a carrotarian!" At that time I would have never guessed that she would eventually become a vegan. It simply demonstrates that if you continuously introduce beautiful, delicious and interesting preparations of a wide variety of veggies even a carrotarian can learn to love them all!

So if you have your own version of a carrotarian, the best tip I can give you is to add yummy compound butters, sauces and flavored oils to entice them and soon enough things will change - their bodies will begin to crave the veggies!

In this section you will find some of my favorite ways to prepare veggies and I predict they may become some of your favorites as well . . .

Black Quinoa, Gingered Peaches, Crisp Snap Peas & Baby Spinach

This beautiful side dish tastes even better than it looks! Black quinoa is an extremely nutritious seed with a nutty flavor and wonderful texture. The sweet peaches absorb the ginger and the brilliant green peas retain their crunch. If it's true that we eat with our eyes first, this beautifully visual dish will be everyone's favorite!
Serves 6

1 cup black quinoa
2 cups pH 9.5 ionized water
1/2 teaspoon Ginger Paste

1 tablespoon Gingery Rice Wine Vinegar
1 tablespoon Peach Balsamic Vinegar
1 1/2 teaspoons San-J GF low sodium tamari
1 tablespoon agave nectar
2 tablespoons lemon juice
1/4 teaspoon ginger paste

2 fresh peaches
1 1/2 cups sugar snap peas
1 scallion
3 cups baby spinach

Rinse quinoa well. Drain and pat dry. Toast in a deep 10 inch skillet until dry. Add water and ginger, cover and bring to a boil. Simmer about 5 minutes then turn heat off, leaving skillet on hot burner to steam. Quinoa will be perfectly cooked in about 20 minutes. Meanwhile, mix vinegars, tamari, agave, lemon juice and ginger paste. Toss with warm quinoa and set aside.

Bring water to a boil, add 1 tablespoon Celtic sea salt. Remove stem end and any tough strings from the peas. Cut on a sharp diagonal into 2-3 pieces each. Drop into boiling water for 3 minutes. Remove and drop into a bowl of iced water to stop the cooking process and retain the bright green color.

Halve peaches and remove pits. Slice each peach into 12 slices then in half again crosswise.
Slice scallion into thin slices.

Gently toss quinoa, peaches, peas and scallions to distribute vinaigrette. Line plates with baby spinach then spoon on your beautiful quinoa. Serve warm or room temperature.

Baby Bok Choy in Orange-Ginger Sauce

This Asian inspired dish is lightly sauced, delicately flavored and beautiful to serve! The ingredient list belies the simplicity of the preparation! In just 10 minutes you have a dish that tastes like it came from your favorite restaurant!
Serves 4

8 baby bok choy halved lengthwise
1 1/2 cups scallions cut on sharp diagonal
1 1/2 inch piece fresh ginger
2 cloves finely minced garlic
1 teaspoon toasted sesame oil
1 teaspoon peanut oil
1 1/2 cups orange juice
1/2 cup vegetable broth
1 1/2 teaspoons low sodium tamari
1 teaspoon arrowroot
1 teaspoon honey
1 pinch red chili flakes
1 orange zested and segmented
1/4 teaspoon black sesame seeds

Using a spoon peel ginger and slice into 3/4 inch long julienned strips. Heat oils over medium-high heat then add ginger and garlic. When lightly browned remove with a slotted spoon. Add orange juice and tamari to skillet and bring to a slow boil and simmer until reduced in half.

In a small bowl mix vegetable broth, arrowroot and honey until smooth. Slowly add to the orange juice and continue to whisk until smooth and slightly thickened. Return garlic and ginger to the mixture then add the bok choy, scallions, chili flakes and about half of the zest, cover and cook until wilted.

Place on a warmed serving plate and sprinkle with orange segments, sesame seeds and remaining zest. Serve immediately.

Smokey Baba Ganoush

This version is made with grilled rather than baked eggplant and grilled lemons. Grilling adds a slight smoky flavor to this creamy, delicious Middle-Eastern favorite! It's surprisingly easy to make and is a great dip for fresh veggies, a spread for sandwiches or a creamy accompaniment to other Middle-Eastern salads.
Yield – 1 1/2 cups

1 large or 2 smaller eggplants, weight totaling about 1 1/2 pounds
3 large garlic cloves finely minced
1/4 cup tahini
1 teaspoon fine lemon zest
3-4 lemons halved, grilled and juiced (1/3 cup juice needed)
1 teaspoon Celtic sea salt
1 teaspoon Middle-Eastern Spice Blend
1/8 teaspoon ground cumin
1/4 teaspoon red pepper flakes (optional)
1 tablespoon olive oil

To grill the eggplant, prick several times with a fork and cook over medium-high heat for approximately 4 minutes on each section of the eggplant. When eggplant is very soft, remove from the heat, cover and cool.

To grill lemons, cut lemons in half, brush cut side very lightly with olive oil and grill until soft, about 3-5 minutes. Set aside to cool slightly before juicing. Grilled lemons generally produce a great deal of juice.

When eggplant is cool enough to work with, cut in half, drain excess juice (reserve) and scoop soft flesh into a food processor. Add lemon juice and zest, tahini, garlic, spices, olive oil and half of the salt. Process until smooth. If too thick you can add 1 tablespoon reserved juice from eggplant. Taste and adjust seasonings.

Spoon into bowl and garnish with a drizzle of olive oil and chopped parsley.

Potato and Veggie Pancakes

A delightful option for potato pancakes using no grains or eggs. The secret is using mashed potatoes as the binder to hold the freshly grated potatoes, carrots and zucchini together.
Serves 4-6

Mashed Potatoes

2 small red potatoes
2 small Yukon gold potatoes
1/4 cup Unsweetened Almond or Silk organic unsweetened soy milk
1 tablespoon butter or Ghee
2 teaspoons Celtic sea salt
1/2 teaspoon freshly ground black pepper

Boil potatoes until fork tender in pH 9.0 ionized water and 1 teaspoon salt. Drain and using an electric mixer whip with remaining salt, pepper, butter and milk. Whipping these types of potatoes develops the starches to create a potato that will act more like glue. Set aside to cool.

Veggie Pancakes

1 cup grated Yukon gold or red potatoes
1/2 cup grated carrots
1/2 cup grated zucchini
1 teaspoon finely minced garlic
1 tablespoon finely chopped scallions
1/4 cup finely chopped Roasted Red Peppers
2 tablespoons Herb Infused Olive Oil

Steam veggies for about 3 minutes, just until slightly tender. Combine all ingredients thoroughly.

Heat oil in a skillet or griddle over medium high heat. For ease in flipping, keep these pancakes a bit small – slightly less than 2 tablespoons batter – flatten out a bit. Cover the skillet until golden brown on the first side. Flip and continue cooking until golden brown. Drain on paper towels.

Serve with your favorite Sour Crème Substitute and snipped chives.

Garnet Yams, Black Kale and Coconut Milk Quinoa

This is a quick and colorful side dish that is so earthy and satisfying you will find yourself making it over and over again. Since yams, kale, coconut milk and quinoa are all on my list of super foods, this is a delicious way to get them all into a single delicious dish. It's so nutrient dense and high in protein it's great as a side dish or a main course with a simple green salad.

Serves 4 – 6

1 cup vegetable broth or water
1 cup Thai Kitchen organic coconut milk
1 cup white quinoa
2 teaspoons Lemon Infused Olive Oil
1 cup finely chopped red or sweet yellow onion
1 teaspoons Ginger Paste
2 tablespoons sliced lemongrass
1 small kaffir lime leaf
1 1/2 cups cubed peeled garnet or jewel yams
1 cup black kale, sliced into ribbons
1 teaspoon chopped fresh thyme leaves
1 teaspoon San J gluten free, low sodium tamari
1/4 teaspoon black pepper
1 1/2 cups cooked black beans
1 tablespoon lime juice

Bring broth (or water), coconut milk, lime leaf (if un-available substitute 1 teaspoon lime zest and add with lime juice at the end of the recipe) and quinoa to a boil in a medium saucepan over medium-high heat. (If you have left over quinoa from breakfast Coconut Quinoa in Fresh Plum Syrup this is a great way to repurpose it! Then place lime leaf in the skillet with the onion to infuse its perfumed flavor.) Cover and boil 5 minutes, turn heat off and leave pan in place 20 minutes or until liquid is absorbed.

Meanwhile heat oil in a large skillet over medium heat and sweat onion until it's translucent. Add yams, kale and 1 table-spoon water, cover and cook until tender, stirring occasionally. When tender carefully stir in black beans and heat through. Add thyme leaves, lime juice, salt and pepper, taste and adjust seasonings if necessary. Carefully stir in quinoa and serve. Garnish with a few sprigs of thyme.

Oven Fried Zucchini Sticks

At the end of the summer growing season most gardeners find they have an abundance of summer squashes, from zucchini to yellow crookneck to patty pan. All delicious and all perfect for this recipe. So if your local neighbor or farmers' market has an abundance at a great price, here is a special treatment that everyone will love! All of the taste of the deep fat fried version without the extra fat and hassle. Serve with a great dipping sauce like Roasted Red Pepper Dip
Yield – about 36

3 medium zucchini in 1/2 x 3 inch sticks
1 tablespoon Celtic sea salt
1 1/4 cups Rice Bread crumbs
1/3 cup freshly grated Romano cheese (optional)
1 tablespoon Bruschetta Spice Blend
1/4 cup any GF flour
2 eggs well beaten or 1/2 cup egg substitute
2 tablespoons Unsweetened Almond or soy milk
Olive oil spray

Place the sticks into a colander over a bowl and sprinkle with salt and drain for 1 hour or longer. The salt will draw out some of the excess water to keep your sticks crispy. Rinse quickly to remove the excess salt then pat dry.

Preheat the oven to 425 degrees. Line a baking sheet with parchment paper and spray lightly with olive oil. Set aside.

In a shallow bowl beat eggs and milk together to create an egg wash. (If using an egg substitute I find that a powder combined with water and flax gel usually works best as an egg wash.) In a separate bowl combine rice bread crumbs, seasoning and cheese.

Toss squash sticks in flour a few at a time, then dip into egg wash, then roll in seasoned bread crumbs. Lay them out on baking sheets, lightly spray with olive oil. Bake 10-12 minutes, or until the bottom is lightly browned, turn over and bake an additional 8-10 minutes.

Transfer to a warm serving platter with a bowl of your favorite dip.

Pan Roasted Potatoes

This is the fastest way to roast potatoes. They are easy to prepare and delicious!
Serves 4

1 pound small red, Yukon or fingerling potatoes
1 tablespoon Herb Infused Olive Oil
1 tablespoon butter or Ghee
1 teaspoon Celtic sea salt
1/4 teaspoon freshly ground black paper
1/4 cup diced red onion
1 finely minced clove garlic
1/4 cup diced red pepper
1 tablespoon chopped fresh rosemary
1/2 teaspoon chopped thyme

In a Dutch oven heat butter and oil. Add thoroughly washed potatoes (choose potatoes that are similar in size to ensure even cooking), salt and pepper. Shake well to evenly distribute potatoes and butter mixture. Cover and cook over medium low heat about 20 minutes, or until almost fork tender. Add onion, garlic and red pepper, shake to distribute and continue cooking for about 5 minutes. Add herbs, cover, shake and turn heat off but leave pot on hot burner. Potatoes will continue to cook until you are ready for them.

Lemon and Herb Roasted Fennel

I love fennel! Its crisp texture and mild anise flavor cannot be replicated and when roasted, they become sweeter and a bit earthy. Very satisfying. Serves 4.

2 large heads fennel, bulb only
2 tablespoons Lemon Infused Olive Oil
1 tablespoons Herb Infused Olive Oil
1/4 teaspoons Italian seasoning
Celtic sea salt and black pepper to taste

Cut fennel bulbs into even 3/4 inch wedges, save the stems and fronds for another use. Mix oils and Italian seasoning in a small bowl and brush over all sides of the fennel. Place on a well-oiled roasting pan or cookie sheet and roast in a 375° for about 40 minutes, turning with a spatula at the half way point and adding a sprinkle of little salt and pepper.

Angela's Quick Polenta Stuffing

My daughter shared this quick side dish she put together one evening. Its flavor is very similar to cornbread dressing but comes together in just minutes by taking advantage of Ancient Harvest's pre-prepared Quinoa Polenta. However, you can use any leftover polenta or even rice "grits" to make this dish. It's colorful, flavorful and completely satisfying!
Serves 4

2 cups polenta cubes
1 cup diced red or sweet yellow onion
3 large carrots diced
4 celery ribs diced
1 tablespoon Garlic Infused Olive Oil
1/4 teaspoon freshly ground black pepper
1/4 teaspoon Celtic sea salt

In an ovenproof skillet over medium heat, sweat onion, carrots and celery in oil until onion is translucent. Add polenta cubes and bake at 350 degrees about 30 minutes or until veggies are tender and polenta is lightly browned.

Basic Rice "Grits"

This basic recipe is so quick, easy and delicious to make. Since corn and its byproducts are allergens for many, and there is so much controversy over GMO's and corn, I developed a recipe that many of you will find more desirable. Even the staunchest Southerner will find these "grits" totally delicious . . . in fact I've served it to several and they did not know they were not traditional hominy grits!
Yield – 1 1/2 cups

1 cup almond or Silk organic unsweetened soy milk
1/3 cup brown rice "farina" style cereal
1/8 Celtic sea salt
1/8 teaspoon freshly ground black pepper
1/8 teaspoon garlic granules
1 tablespoon butter or ghee

Bring milk, salt and garlic to a boil, slowly whisk brown rice cereal in until fully incorporated. Continue to stir until cereal is thick. Cover and remove from heat. Let it stand for 5 minutes, stir in black pepper and butter until smooth.

Cheesy "Grits"

While I adore the flavor of corn, I am well aware of all the controversy over GMO corn on the market. Whenever possible I opt for blue corn but sometimes that leaves a dish looking a bit odd . . . So for all of you Southerners and anyone who has visited the Deep South and was introduced to hominy grits here is a great option! No corn but tons of flavor, and since hominy grits are creamy white in color, no one will suspect you've made the switch.
 Serves 4

3 cups Unsweetened Almond Milk
2 teaspoon vegetable bouillon
1 1/2 cups rice cereal
1/3 cup shredded Romano cheese*
1/3 cup crumbled goat cheese*
Pinch of cayenne and black pepper

In a heavy bottomed 2 quart sauce pan heat milk and bouillon to a low boil. Slowly whisk in the rice cereal and bring back to a boil. Reduce the heat and continue to stir until thick – about 6 minutes. Remove from heat and stir in the pepper and cheeses.

Serve family style in a large heated bowl as a complement to roasted veggies, poached eggs, seafood or chicken.

Basic Rice "Polenta"

I am a big fan of polenta. I think in the South grits have always been popular, but in areas of the country where there was more Italian influence polenta has always reigned supreme. With the introduction of GMO's to corn crops it has gotten much more difficult to find non-GMO and organic corn products. However, that doesn't mean that you have live without all those great polenta based dishes. Here is a great substitute I think you will love . . .
Yield – 1 1/2 cups

1 cup pH 9.5 ionized water
1/3 cup brown rice "farina" style cereal
Pinch of Celtic sea salt
2 tsp nutritional yeast
2 tsp butter
1/2 teaspoon Italian seasoning

Bring water and salt to a boil over medium heat, slowly whisk in brown rice cereal until fully incorporated. Stir in butter, nutritional yeast and Italian seasoning until cereal is thick. Remove from heat, pour into a flat pan to cool about 5 minutes or until set. Cut into triangles or squares, or into specialty shapes with cookie cutters, and serve. For grilled or sautéed polenta, chill at least 1 hour, then grill or sauté.

Cheesy Polenta

There are several styles of polenta, some are thick and some are creamy. This one is an anomaly because it's both very thick and very creamy. I developed it specifically for Peidmontese Peppers but use it for everything from pizza crusts to toasted cubes for salads.
Yield - 8 servings

1 cup organic coarse polenta
1 cup Homemade Vegetable Stock
1 1/2 cups pH 9.5 ionized water
1 tablespoons butter or Ghee
2 oz blue cheese crumbled
1 oz Romano cheese
Celtic sea salt and freshly ground pepper

In a heavy bottomed sauce pot bring stock and water to a rolling boil. Slowly add polenta stirring constantly until smooth and polenta begins to pull away from the sides of the pot, about 20 minutes.

Add butter, mix thoroughly, fold in cheeses and season to taste. Spread out on a damp cutting board and cool. Cut into 4 squares, transfer to a parchment lined baking sheet and broil until cheese melts and begins to bubble.

Transfer polenta to warmed dinner plates, top with peppers and serve with a fresh arugula tossed with the remaining dressing as a great side salad.

Vegan Cheezy Polenta

Substitute Garlic Infused Olive Oil for the butter, instead of blue cheese use Cashew Goat Cheeze, and substitute crumbled Almond Feta Cheeze for the Romano and add 1/2 cup grated rice mozzarella to add the gooey factor.

Sweet Potato Hash with Pepitas

This is a perfect side dish for any informal meal. Deep orange yams, green pepitas, red bell peppers, yellow onions and fresh herbs make this dish both beautiful and nutrient dense. Each component of the dish is delicious on it's own, but when combined they create a total feast for the senses. This hash is so versatile that it is equally at home with eggs at breakfast, black bean burgers at lunch or Oven Fried Chicken at dinner. I love this hash with steamed kale . . . I can hardly get enough!

Serves 4

6 cups diced garnet yams
1 cup diced yellow onion
1 cup diced red bell pepper
2 tablespoons finely diced shallot
1 teaspoon minced garlic
2 teaspoons Spicy Southwestern Infused Oil
2 teaspoons butter
1/4 cup pepitas
1/4 teaspoon crushed red pepper flakes
1/4 teaspoon Celtic sea salt
1/4 teaspoon freshly ground black pepper
1/2 teaspoon fresh thyme leaves

Soak pepitas in pH 11.5 ionized water* 20 minutes, drain well and set aside.

In a heavy bottomed skillet over medium heat, sweat onions, red pepper, shallot and garlic until onions 3-4 minutes. Add remaining ingredients, 1 tablespoon water, cover and cook 5 minutes. With a thin metal spatula turn veggies over to brown the other side and cook uncovered until yams are tender, turning every 3-4 minutes.

Serve as a side dish sprinkled with thyme leaves or chopped cilantro.

Roasted Heirloom Tomatoes

As a little girl I loved tomatoes so much that my Mom always gave me the first ripe tomato of the summer . . . still warm from the sun, perfectly balanced sweet and acidic, it was the height of the garden season for me. I still feel the same, and I still look forward to my first heirloom tomato every summer! And roasting tomatoes brings out the best in these delicious fruits of summer. The flavors concentrate and they get even more delicious and cooking actually increases the availability of a very important nutrient, lycopene! So when you have an abundance of tomatoes, go ahead and roast a few and you can enjoy them in so many ways!
Serves 4

2 pounds ripe heirloom tomatoes – I like to use a variety of sizes and colors
2 tablespoons Herb Infused Olive Oil
1/2 teaspoon Tuscan Sea Salt Blend
1/2 teaspoon freshly ground black pepper
1/2 teaspoon thyme leaves
1/2 teaspoon rosemary leaves
2 teaspoons basil ribbons
12 basil sprigs
1 teaspoon finely minced garlic

Preheat oven to 400 degrees.

Place tomatoes on a rimmed baking sheet and brush with oil. In a small bowl mix herbs, garlic salt and pepper. Sprinkle over tomatoes.   Bake about 15 minutes or until tomatoes are soft, but still hold their shape.

There are so many ways to serve these delicious tomatoes! Let your imagination be your guide.

Saffron Rice

Brilliantly yellow, aromatic and bursting with nutrition, this rice is a wonderful part of many Spanish, South American, East Indian and Mediterranean dishes. Turmeric is a powerful antioxidant, brown rice is packed with vitamins and minerals and coconut oil provides all important medium chain fatty acids. All this and it tastes so nutty and delicious! Add in some brilliant green snap peas and red bell peppers and it looks more like art than food!
Yield – 3 cups

1 cup brown basmati rice
2 cups pH 9.5 water
2 pinches saffron threads
1 teaspoon turmeric
1/4 teaspoon salt
1 tablespoon coconut oil

Rinse rice until the water is clear then drain in a colander until dry. Meanwhile measure water and "bloom" the saffron threads in the water for at least 30 minutes.

Heat coconut oil in medium saucepan, add rice and turmeric and toast lightly. This step helps to keep your rice separate and it enhances the flavor of the rice. Add saffron water, bring to a boil, reduce heat to low, cover and leave it alone (this is very hard for me so I use a glass lid so I can still watch it) until all of the water is absorbed.   Remove from heat, leave the lid on and let it stand for about 5 minutes. Remove the lid, fluff with a fork. Transfer to serving bowl and garnish with a few toasted fennel seeds and a bit of chopped cilantro or parsley.

While white basmati rice will produce a much more vibrantly colored rice and it cooks a little faster, it has been stripped of its bran. The bran is the portion of the rice that is packed with minerals. Additionally, the texture of brown rice is a little chewier and the flavor a little nuttier. All-in-all brown rice is an outstanding flavor, texture and nutritional choice in this dish!

Mediterranean Style Sautéed Veggies

This is a flavor packed way to serve fresh veggies that are available all year long. The salty, tangy, intense flavors of the olives, sundried tomatoes and feta are mellowed by the mild flavors of the veggies. You will love this and it takes only a few minutes to make an impressive side dish. If you like it's also great tossed with a few No-Knead Ciabatta croutons or served over pasta spirals and peppery arugula to make a main dish out of this beautiful array of veggies.
Serves 4

2 cups Tuscan kale in 1/4 inch ribbons
1 cup zucchini cut on sharp diagonal
1 cup yellow squash cut on sharp diagonal
1 medium red pepper, julienned
3 tablespoons sliced shallots
1 clove garlic, minced
1/4 cup oil packed sundried tomatoes, chopped
6-8 kalamata olives halved
4-6 green Greek olives halved
3 sprigs fresh thyme
1 tablespoon Sundried Tomato Infused Olive Oil
2 tablespoons Marinated Feta

Heat 2 teaspoons of the oil over medium heat. Add shallots and cook just until they begin to brown. Add red pepper, zucchini and yellow squash. Season with a generous sprinkle of salt and pepper. Cook veggies until they begin to brown slightly but are still crisp tender.

Meanwhile, add remaining olive oil, sundried tomatoes, thyme leaves and olives to a bowl. When the veggies are finished, add to the bowl and toss then sprinkle with cheese. The heat of the veggies warms the tomatoes and olives. Serve hot or at room temperature.

To turn this into a main dish, simply toss with 2 cups of baby arugula and 2 cups of either No Knead Ciabatta croutons or 2 cups of your favorite pasta. This main dish contains leafy greens, a starch and your veggies . . . who could ask for an easier and more satisfying dinner . . .

Spicy Mustard Greens with Confetti Pan Roasted Potatoes with Lemon-Tahini Sauce

This is a quick easy dish that you can serve as a side dish or a vegetarian main dish. Mustard greens are so spicy and slightly bitter so the creamy potatoes are a wonderful contrast. When topped with the silky lemon and tahini sauce this is a perfect combination of slightly sweet, bitter, tangy and spicy. Since both the tahini and greens are excellent sources of calcium and magnesium and the potatoes are high in potassium this is a delicious way to get a big boost in some very important minerals! (Photo, page 120)
Yield – 4 side dish servings or 2 main dish servings

6 cups mustard greens cut into 1 x 2 inch strips
1 cup mustard green stems chopped into 1/4 inch pieces
1 1/2 pounds mixed baby potatoes
1 tablespoon Herb Infused Olive Oil
1 pinch Celtic sea salt and cracked black pepper
3 tablespoons tahini
5 tablespoons lemon juice
1/2 teaspoon lemon zest
1/4 teaspoon granulated garlic
1/2 teaspoon ginger paste

To pan roast your baby potatoes, simply wash potatoes and add to a sauce pot with a tight fitting lid. Add olive oil, 1 tablespoon water, salt and pepper and cook over medium heat about 15 minutes shaking pan every 5 minutes. Add mustard green stems to the pot, shake and continue to cook until potatoes are fork tender.

Meanwhile, place mustard greens in a large, high sided skillet with a tightly fitting lid. Add water until it is 1 inch deep and cook over medium high heat about 15 minutes. Greens should be dark green, soft and only slightly bitter. If greens are undercooked they will be quite bitter, so a taste test is the best way to determine when they are ready to remove from the pot.

While the potatoes and greens are cooking combine the tahini, lemon juice and zest, garlic and ginger (if you do not have the paste simply grate fresh ginger on a microplane). Mix well and taste. Add more lemon juice or garlic to taste.
Mound greens on a warmed serving plate. Halve potatoes and toss on the greens. Drizzle dressing over the greens and potatoes. Garnish with crispy stems and serve.

Smashed Potatoes with Chiles, Chives and Chili-Lime Crema

This is a cross between a warm potato salad and a potato skins appetizer. Topped with flavor packed, high protein Cilantro-Lime Crème and laced with fresh chives and spicy chilies these are bound to become a favorite dish at your next picnic or patio party! Serve them with your favorite grilled meat or veggies or use slightly smaller potatoes and pass on a tray for a casual hors d'oeuvers.
Serves 4

8 small red potatoes, approximately 2 inches in diameter
2 cloves garlic
1 tablespoon Celtic sea salt
1 tablespoon seeded and minced fresno, red jalapeno or red serrano
Chives cut into 2 inch pieces
Roasted red bell pepper cut into inch long pieces
1/3 cup Chile-Lime Crema

Scrub potatoes, place in a large pot and cover with pH 9.5 ionized water, add salt and garlic cloves. Bring to a boil and cook until fork tender. Drain and return to hot pot for about 5 minutes. This step helps the potatoes dry out a bit so they soak up the liquids and flavors from the topping.

Transfer to a serving tray and smash with the heal of your hand. The potatoes will still have some shape. Remove any skin from the center of the potato and sprinkle with 1/8 to ¼ teaspoon minced peppers and press them into the potato a bit (the peppers can be omitted for a mild version of this dish).

Top with Cilantro-Lime Crème and garnish with chives and peppers. Serve hot or at room temperature.

Rainbow Swiss Chard, Basil and Pine Nuts in Lemon Butter

I've always liked the combination of the crunchy ribs and the tender leaves of Swiss chard. This recipe takes advantage of both in a buttery lemon and garlic sauce.

The aromatic and creamy pine nuts and smooth flavor of basil and sharp flavor of pecorino cheese, gives you all the best flavors of a pesto without the effort.

Serves 3-4

1 tablespoon butter
2 teaspoons olive oil
1 large bunch rainbow Swiss chard
¼ cup diced red onion
2 cloves minced garlic
2 teaspoons lemon zest
1 small lemon juiced
1 small handful basil
2 large pinches Celtic sea salt and freshly ground black pepper
2 tablespoons toasted pine nuts
Shaved pecorino cheese or Almond Feta Crumbles

Preheat oven to 300 degrees. Spread pine nuts on a small sheet and roast until golden. Set aside.

Thoroughly clean chard, removed the ribs and set leaves aside. Thinly slice ribs. Cut leaves in half lengthwise. Stack leaves and slice into narrow ribbons.

Stack basil leaves, roll and slice into thin ribbons and set aside.

Heat a large, heavy bottomed skillet to medium heat. Add olive oil and butter. When butter is melted and begins to bubble add lemon juice, half the zest, diced onion, minced garlic and sliced chard ribs. Sprinkle with salt and pepper. Saute until onions are translucent, stirring frequently to ensure the garlic does not brown.

To the skillet add basil and about half of the chard ribbons and toss to coat, then add the remainder and toss once again. Cover and allow to steam-saute about 1 minute. Turn and repeat. When chard is wilted, tender and still brightly colored, transfer to a warmed serving plate. Top with toasted pine nuts and cheese. Serve immediately.

Spinach with Chili, Lime and Garlic

This Southwestern inspired twist on a super star of greens is very delicious and pairs perfectly with your favorite south of the border dishes.
Serves 2

5 cups baby spinach
2 cloves garlic, crushed and roughly chopped
1 teaspoon lime zest
1 teaspoon lime juice
1/4 teaspoon red chili flakes
1/4 teaspoon sea salt
2 teaspoons Spicy Southwestern Chili Infused Olive Oil

Heat oil and lightly sauté garlic. Add spinach, lime juice, lime zest, chili flakes and salt. Cook just until wilted. Taste and adjust seasonings. Place on a warm serving tray.

Nutritional Note: Potatoes have been considered the enemy of healthy eating by many, but they are actually high in potassium, magnesium, phosphorus, calcium, manganese, fiber, as well as vitamins B and C, plus protein! Generally the problem lies in what we choose to put on or in them. These recipes maximize both taste and nutrition!

MAIN DISHES

The star of any meal can be made from very humble to ultra-exotic ingredients. A main dish can be simple or simply elegant depending upon how you prepare and serve it.

But they all begin the same . . . with clean yet complex flavors, colors and textures. When you work with fresh, high quality ingredients your main dishes will always be stand outs!

This section is filled with some of my favorites. From a most unusual grainless pizza, to cornless grits, and the tastiest coconut tofu, from veggies to seafood to chicken and tempe this section contains some of the best main dish recipes I've ever developed!

So whether your choice is fish, fowl, veggies or grains you will find dishes that satisfy your taste buds, your wallet and your soul. And because I believe that it's completely unnecessary to sacrifice taste for nutrition, I have designed each recipe to maximize nutritional value without sacrificing flavor!

So go ahead grab your chef's apron and take a walk on the wild side!

5 Cheese and Roasted Veggie Pizza on a Potato Crust

This is one of the best pizzas I have ever made! The crisp potato crust is the perfect bed for roasted cherry tomatoes, bell peppers, caramelized shallots, tender young zucchini, sautéed mushrooms and fresh herbs . . . not to mention the variety of goat and sheep's milk cheeses. You will not be disappointed! Best of all with only a few refrigerator basics it takes only seconds to throw together. When entertaining, make 4 smaller crusts and allow your friends to customize their toppings.
Yield – 4 entrée or 16 appetizer portions

1 Crispy Potato Crust
1 pint cherry tomatoes, halved
1/4 each red, yellow and orange bell pepper
1 small zucchini
1 shallot
4-5 crimini mushrooms
2 ounces fresh goat cheese
1 ounce goat mozzarella
2 ounces Romano
1 ounce Ricotta Substitute
1 ounce pecorino
2 sprigs thyme
1 small sprig rosemary
2 teaspoons chopped parsley
6 basil leaves
Salt and pepper
1/2 teaspoon Italian seasoning
4 teaspoons olive oil plus olive oil spray

Preheat broiler.

Roasting and caramelizing all veggies intensifies the flavors as well as reducing the water content so your crust will not get soggy. Place cherry tomato halves and peppers, skin side up, on a baking sheet, sprinkle lightly with salt, pepper and Italian seasoning. Spray tomatoes with a little olive oil and place under broiler until the skin on the peppers is blistered and black. Remove from oven and set oven to 400 degrees. Place peppers in a glass bowl with a lid for 5-10 minutes before removing skins. Julienne and set aside.

Using a mandoline, thinly slice shallots and zucchini. Strip leaves from thyme and rosemary, tear basil leaves, set aside.

Slice mushrooms, sauté in 2 teaspoons olive oil and a sprinkle of Italian seasoning until golden, remove from pan and set aside. Add remaining olive oil and shallots, stir, lower heat and cover. Cook until caramelized, about 6-8 minutes. Remove and add zucchini, sprinkle with salt and pepper and cook until tender, about 4 minutes, remove and set aside. Finely grate pecorino, Romano and mozzarella then set aside. Crumble fresh goat cheese, add Ricotta Substitute and mix lightly.

Now you are ready to assemble your pizza. Sprinkle on the cheeses, reserving the Romano, top with roasted and caramelized veggies, top with Romano and bake until all ingredients are heated and cheese has melted, about 10 minutes. Remove and top with herbs. Cut into pieces and enjoy!

Crispy Potato Pizza Crust

This is one of the best pizza crusts I've ever made, but them I'm an Irish girl so give me a potato and I'll generally love it! The interesting twist is that it is not only GF it's also completely Grain Free and yet it maintains some of my favorite pizza crust components . . . it's crisp yet chewy, light and flavorful.
Yield – 11 x 15 inch crust

2 pounds baking potatoes
Olive oil spray
1/2 teaspoon Celtic sea salt
1/2 teaspoon freshly ground black pepper
1/2 teaspoon Italian seasoning

Move rack to the bottom of the oven then preheat to 400 degrees. Using a medium microplane or box grater, grate potatoes into a bowl of iced water. This step will remove a lot of starch as well as keep the potatoes from turning brown. Remove potatoes from the water one handful at a time. Squeeze as much water out of each handful as possible. Spread out on 2 layers of kitchen towels. Roll the towels and twist to wring out any remaining water.

Line a baking sheet with parchment paper then lightly spray with olive oil. Spread potatoes evenly, about 1/8 to 1/4 inch thickness. Sprinkle salt, pepper and herbs over potatoes then lightly spray with olive oil.

Bake about 25 minutes or until the potatoes are crisp and lightly browned. Remove, add toppings of your choice and return to oven to reheat.

Baked 5 Cheese Pasta Penne with Cherry Tomatoes and Tuscan Kale

I have always loved fancy macaroni and cheese dishes and this one does not disappoint! It's creamy and the pasta is perfectly al dente, the veggies are bright, colorful and when paired they pack a nutritional punch. This tastes like a version filled with tons of fat and empty calories, but it is neither of those . . . so give it a try! I used VitaSpelt Penne in this dish but you can easily substitute Einkorn or GF Bionaturae Fusilli, or GF Ancient Harvest Quinoa Shells. Terrific with just a fresh salad.
Serves 4

2 cups uncooked pasta
4 cups Tuscan black kale in ribbons
1 pint cherry tomatoes halved
1/4 cup red onion diced
1 clove garlic, minced
1 cup rice bread crumbs
1 teaspoon Herb Infused Olive Oil
1 teaspoon fresh thyme leaves plus sprigs for garnish
1/4 teaspoon Celtic sea salt
1/4 teaspoon black pepper
2 cups 5 Cheese Sauce
2 tablespoons freshly grated Romano

Bring 6 cups pH 9.5 ionized water to a rolling boil. Add 1 tablespoon Celtic sea salt, and the pasta. Cook for half the recommended time, it will finish cooking in the oven.

Drain and mix with kale, tomatoes, onions and sauce. Turn out into a buttered 8 x 8 casserole dish.
Toss breadcrumbs with oil and thyme leaves, salt and pepper. Spread over the pasta and bake for about 30 minutes or until the sauce is bubbling, top is golden and pasta is perfectly tender. Garnish with fresh thyme sprigs and cheese.

Lemon, Caper and Dill Halibut or Salmon

This is a quick and easy, yet wonderfully flavorful. This is one of those entrees that's perfect anytime you need a high protein, quick to prepare meal! The taste is indistinguishable from the same dish prepared at your favorite French restaurant, but this version contains about ¼ the fat and calories! I use it in my Updated Salade Niçoise, but it's so versatile you can serve it as an entrée with steamed veggies and a quick salad.
Serves 4

1 1/4 pounds skinless wild caught Alaskan salmon or halibut filets
1 tablespoon butter or Ghee
1/3 cup Lemon, Caper and Dill Marinade and Sauce
1 teaspoon capers
Lemon slices and dill sprigs for garnish

Remove any skin and pin bones from fish. Rinse and pat dry. Lightly season both sides of fish with a sprinkle of salt and pepper. Place in a glass container and pour marinade over. Marinate about 15 minutes, turning over 1 time to be certain all sides of the fish have been adequately exposed to the marinade.

Using medium heat, melt butter in a sauté pan that has a lid. Place fish in the center of the pan and pour marinade over. Cover and cook to desired temperature, turning half way through. Depending upon the thickness of your cut, 1-3 minutes per side.

Remove from heat, transfer to heated serving platter. Pour pan sauce over fish. Garnish with fresh dill, thin lemon slices and a sprinkle of capers. Serve immediately.

Mock Halibut in Lemon, Caper and Dill Sauce

This is a nice treatment of tofu that closely resembles halibut. The kelp granules impart the unmistakable, and completely delicious taste of the sea while providing iodine that's generally missing from the average vegan diet. It makes a great main dish, a fantastic sandwich or the star of a beautiful salad.
Serves 2

1 package organic extra firm tofu
1 teaspoon kelp granules
1/4 teaspoon Mediterranean Salt Blend
1/2 cup Lemon, Caper and Dill Marinade and Sauce
1 teaspoon rough chopped dill plus sprigs for garnish
1 teaspoon coarse lemon zest
4 lemon slices
1 teaspoon capers

Freeze, defrost and press tofu. Slice into 4 thick steaks. Arrange in a broiler proof baking dish with a small space between steaks. Sprinkle with kelp and salt, pour Lemon, Caper and Dill Marinade and Sauce over, cover and marinate overnight, turning once to be sure all surfaces are covered with marinade. Bring to room temperature then broil until tofu is lightly browned, turn and brown on all sides, sauce will thicken slightly.

To serve place tofu on a warmed serving platter, pour sauce over, garnish with dill, lemon slices and capers.

Nutrition Note: Iodine is a natural antidepressant because it increases the uptake of tryptophan, which in turn, converts to mood stabilizing serotonin.

Crispy GF Coconut Chicken

I love crunchy coconut coating and the great news is that rice bread makes THE best breadcrumbs . . . these crumbs are crisp, brown perfectly and don't soak up oil. So no need to give up the crunch especially when combined with coconut shreds. This combo is so cruchalicious!!! To get it to stick and provide a wonderful subtle flavor I created a coconut marinade that I think you will love as much as I do! Serve with your favorite dipping sauces.
Serves 4

1 cup Coconut Marinade
1 1/2 pounds boneless, skinless chicken breast or chicken strips
2 cups organic coconut shreds
1 cup Rice Bread crumbs made from about 4 slices of slightly stale or lightly toasted bread
1/4 cup coconut oil
1 1/2 teaspoons Celtic sea salt
1 teaspoon freshly ground pepper

I prefer to use chicken breasts rather than chicken strips so I can cut them just a bit thicker. This ensures they will cook evenly and stay moist. Cut chicken breasts lengthwise into 3/4 inch thick strips. Sprinkle with approximately half of the salt and pepper then coat thoroughly with Coconut Marinade. Cover and refrigerate at least 2 hours to overnight. The marinade will not only flavor the chicken and act as the "glue" to adhere the breading, the enzymes in the yogurt act as a tenderizer and the coconut milk keeps the chicken moist. Remove from refrigerator and sit in a warm place for 10-30 minutes.

In a food processor pulse bread slices until they are uniform crumbs. Add coconut, salt and pepper and pulse to thoroughly combine. Place in a shallow pan or bowl. Working with 1 strip at a time, remove from marinade, making sure all sides are well coated. Press all sides in coconut breading and set aside until all strips are well coated.

In a large frying pan heat coconut oil over a medium-high heat. Oil is hot enough when a bit of the breading crackles a bit when dropped in the oil along the outside edge of the skillet. Working quickly, carefully place strips in oil leaving a bit of room around all sides. Cook until golden, turn and continue to cook until golden brown. If your skillet is too small to accommodate all your strips at one time, cook in small batches and keep in a warm oven until all strips are fully cooked.

Place on a warm platter and serve immediately with Raspbenero Dipping Sauce or Mango Salsa.

Crispy GF Oven Fried Coconut Tofu

I love crunchy coconut coating and the great news is that rice bread makes THE best bread crumbs . . . these crumbs are crisp and brown perfectly in the oven! So if you are looking for a lighter version of a coconut breaded dish, this is it! A light spray with coconut oil on each side ensures a crunchalicious coating that is sure to please even non-tofu lovers! It does take a bit of planning since there are several steps to this dish, but I think you will find it worth the wait. It's so delicious I prefer it to Coconut Chicken . . . be sure to serve with generous portions of your favorite spicy dipping sauces.
Serves 4

1 cup Coconut Marinade made with double the spices
2 packages extra firm organic tofu, frozen, defrosted and pressed
2 cups organic coconut shreds
1 cup Rice Bread crumbs made from about 4 slices of slightly stale or lightly toasted bread
2 teaspoons Celtic sea salt
1 teaspoon freshly ground pepper
Coconut oil spray

I have found that the most effective way to remove water from tofu is to freeze and defrost it. It becomes rather spongy and you can literally wring the excess water out. The resulting texture is a bit meatier and allows this oven fried dish to remain crispy. In fact the cold left overs remain a bit crispy. Slice tofu into 1/2 inch steaks, sprinkle with approximately half of the salt and pepper and coat generously with marinade, turning to ensure all surfaces are covered. Marinate 8-24 hours.

The marinade will not only provide flavor, it is the "glue" to adhere the breading, the enzymes in the yogurt provide a tang and the coconut milk replaces some of the water removed from the tofu and keeps it perfectly moist. Remove from refrigerator and bring to room temperature while preparing coating.

Pre-heat oven to 400 degrees. Spray a baking sheet with coconut oil and set aside.

Meanwhile, in a food processor pulse bread slices until they are uniform crumbs. Add coconut, salt and pepper and pulse to thoroughly combine. Place in a shallow pan or bowl. Working with 1 piece at a time, carefully remove from marinade, making sure all sides are still thickly coated. Dredge all sides in coconut breading pressing to ensure a thick coating. Place steaks on sheet, leaving a bit of space on all sides. Spray tops and sides with a very light coating of coconut oil. Bake in the top 1/3 of a hot oven until golden brown. Remove from baking sheet, place on a warm platter and serve with Rasbenero Dipping Sauce for a sweet and spicy kick.

 ## Crispy GF Coconut Halibut

This is a wonderful alternative to Coconut Chicken! The coating is light and crispy and the fish is moist and perfectly, yet subtly spiced. I love to serve with spicy dipping sauces as a counterbalance to the sweetness of the coconut.
Serves 4

1 cup Coconut Marinade
1 to 1 ½ pounds skinless halibut 1/2 to 3/4 inch thick
2 cups organic coconut shreds
1 cup Rice Bread crumbs made from about 4 slices of slightly stale bread
1/4 cup coconut oil
1 teaspoon Celtic sea salt
1 teaspoon freshly ground pepper

Cut halibut into 1 inch strips. Sprinkle with approximately half of the salt and pepper then coat thoroughly with Coconut Marinade. Cover and marinate 30-40 minutes. The lime juice in the marinade will react with fish and begin to "cook" it if left in the marinade more than 40 minutes. The marinade is thick and will not only flavor the fish it also acts as the "glue" to adhere the breading, the enzymes in the yogurt act as a tenderizer and the coconut milk keeps the fish moist.

In a food processor pulse bread slices until they are uniform crumbs. Add coconut, salt and pepper and pulse to thoroughly combine. Place in a shallow pan or bowl. Working with 1 strip at a time, remove from marinade, making sure all sides are well coated. Press all sides in coconut breading and set aside until all strips are well coated.

In a large frying pan heat coconut oil over a medium-high heat. Oil is hot enough when a bit of the breading crackles a bit when dropped in the oil along the outside edge of the skillet. Working quickly, carefully place strips in oil leaving a bit of room around all sides. Cook until golden, turn and continue to cook just until golden brown. Do not overcook the fish. If your skillet is too small to accommodate all your strips at one time, cook in small batches and keep in a warm oven until all strips are fully cooked.

Place on a warm platter and serve immediately with Raspbenero Dipping Sauce or sweet and spicy Mango Salsa.

Crispy GF Coconut Eggplant

I love crunchy coconut coating on eggplant and this combo is almost addictive. It is a great veggie alternative to chicken or fish and the rice bread crumbs help to ensure the eggplant does not soak up too much frying oil. While the chicken, halibut and tofu versions are more tropical in their flavor, eggplant takes the dish in a more Indian direction so I prefer a spicy tomato based dipping sauce like Spicy Tomato Chutney.
Serves 4

1 1/2 cups Coconut Marinade
4 -6 small Japanese or 1 large eggplant
2 1/2 cups organic coconut shreds
1 1/4 cups Rice Bread crumbs made from about 5 slices of slightly stale bread
1 tablespoon Celtic sea salt
1 teaspoon freshly ground pepper
1/4 teaspoon chili flakes
1/4 cup coconut oil

Slice eggplant into 3/4 inch thick slices or rounds, sprinkle generously with about 2 teaspoons salt and place in a colander to drain for at least 30 minutes to 2 hours. Rinsing in pH 9.5 ionized water will remove excess salt and any remaining bitterness. Pat dry and sprinkle lightly with about half of the remaining salt, half of the black pepper and the chili flakes. Coat generously on both sides with Coconut Marinade cover and marinate 1 hour to overnight. The marinade will not only provide flavor, it is the "glue" to adhere the breading, the enzymes in the yogurt provide a tang and the coconut milk keeps the eggplant perfectly moist. Remove from refrigerator and allow to warm slightly while preparing coating – 10-30 minutes.

In a food processor pulse bread slices until they are uniform crumbs. Add coconut, salt and pepper and pulse to thoroughly combine. Place in a shallow pan or bowl. Working with 1 piece at a time, remove from marinade, making sure all sides are well coated. Press all sides in coconut breading and set aside until well coated.

In a large frying pan heat coconut oil over a medium-high heat. Oil is hot enough when a bit of the breading crackles a bit when dropped in the oil along the outside edge of the skillet. Working quickly, carefully place in oil leaving a bit of room around all sides. Cook until golden, turn and continue to cook until golden brown. Cook in small batches and keep in a warm oven until all strips are fully cooked.

Place on a warm platter and serve immediately with Spicy Tomato Chutney or your favorite spicy dipping sauces.

Crispy GF Oven Fried Chicken

My mother made the best fried chicken I've ever eaten, and this oven baked version is a great alternative! The chicken is succulent, the coating is crisp and crunchy and clean up a breeze! The two big secrets are marinating the chicken in a flavorful buttermilk substitute and rice bread crumbs!   I think once you have tried it it will become one of your favorite ways to prepare chicken.

Serves 4

Marinade
1 cup goat or sheep's milk yogurt or Buttermilk Substitute
2 teaspoon sea salt
1 teaspoon freshly ground black pepper
1 teaspoon Italian seasoning
4 small to medium chicken breasts, lightly pounded

Seasoned Bread Crumbs
2 1/2 cups Rice Bread processed into crumbs
1/2 teaspoon Celtic sea salt
1/2 teaspoon freshly ground pepper
Olive oil spray

Blend yogurt, herbs and spices. Thoroughly coat all sides of the chicken with yogurt blend and marinate at least 2 hours and up to 24 hours.

In a food processor pulse bread slices until they are uniform crumbs. Add salt and pepper and pulse to thoroughly combine. Place in a shallow pan or bowl. Working with 1 breast at a time, remove from marinade, making sure all sides are thickly coated in seasoned crumbs.

Spray baking sheet with olive oil and arrange to allow plenty of space between pieces. Set aside, uncovered, to dry about 30 minutes.

Preheat oven to 400 degrees. Lightly spray chicken with olive oil. Bake until golden brown, about 20-25 minutes. Transfer to a warm platter and serve with your favorite side dishes and a salad for a real Southern meal!

Roasted Tomato Tart with a Cornmeal and Rosemary Crust

This is a surprisingly light, yet satisfying dish. Roasting the tomatoes concentrates their flavor and the cornmeal crust is the perfect texture to accompany the cheesy filling. It's great served hot or room temperature. This is one of my favorite easy entertaining dishes.
Yield – 7 x 9 inch tart

1 uncooked 7 x 9 inch Cornmeal and Rosemary Tart Shell
2/3 cup Ricotta Substitute
1 teaspoon nutritional yeast
1/8 teaspoon Celtic sea salt
1/4 teaspoon coarse black pepper
1/2 teaspoon Garlic Paste
2 eggs
1 ounce grated pecorino (about 3/4 cup)
1 ounce grated goat's milk mozzarella
1 ounce grated Romano
2 ounces goat cheese crumbled
2 cups Roasted Tomatoes
1 teaspoon Basil Infused Olive Oil
1/4 cup torn basil leaves

Preheat oven to 375 degrees. Line tart pan bottom with parchment paper.

In a medium sized mixing bowl, beat eggs until thick and yellow, add salt, pepper, garlic, nutritional yeast and Ricotta substitute and beat until light. Pour into Cornmeal and Rosemary Tart Shell. Top with other cheeses, then the Roasted Tomatoes, brush with Basil Oil.

Bake about 25 minutes or until crust is golden brown and center of tart is set. Cool slightly then remove the sides of the tart pan. As you slide the tart on to a serving tray, pull back the parchment paper to remove it. Sprinkle with basil leaves. Cut into desired sizes and serve either warm or room temperature.

Spicy Shrimp over Cheesy "Grits"

Shrimp and Grits is a very traditional southern dish. Generally laden with heavy cream, sour cream and cheddar cheese, this option takes advantage of all of the traditional flavors of this dish with a healthy twist . . . creamy goat cheese and ultra nutritious rice cereal to replace hominy grits. All of the flavor with none of the guilt! Serve with a crisp green salad and you will have a dinner everyone will ask for again and again . . .
Serves 4

1 lb large shrimp, peeled, deveined tails in tact
2 tablespoon lemon infused olive oil
3 tablespoons butter
1 teaspoon vegetable bouillon
1/2 cup red onion diced into 1/4 inch pieces
1 tablespoon finely diced garlic
1 tablespoon finely diced jalapeno pepper
1 cup diced red bell pepper
1 tsp chipotle chili powder
1/2 teaspoon ancho chili powder
1/2 cup lime juice
1/4 cup pH 9.5 Ionized Water
1 teaspoon lime zest
1 teaspoon cumin
1 tablespoon roughly chopped cilantro
2 teaspoon red pepper flakes
1/4 cup sliced green onions

Peel and de-vein shrimp leaving tails intact. Rinse and drain.

In a heavy bottomed skillet melt butter over medium-low heat. Add oil, bouillon, onions, garlic and peppers. Cook, stirring occasionally until the onions are translucent and begin to caramelize on the edges. Add lime juice, cumin, red pepper flakes and water. Bring to a low boil. Add shrimp green onions, lime zest and cilantro. Cook just until the shrimp are pink, about 4 minutes or less. Avoid overcooking.

Place Cheesy "Grits" in the bottom of 4 shallow bowls, divide shrimp between the bowls, pour sauce over the shrimp and grits. Garnish with a few fresh cilantro leaves.

Baby Artichokes over Cheesy "Grits"

In the South shrimp and grits are even found on fancy restaurant menus. So as not to leave out the vegetarians or those allergic to shellfish, here is a beautiful rendition I think everyone can enjoy! (Photo, page 140)
Serves 4

Cheesy "Grits"
12 baby artichokes
1/3 cup finely diced red bell pepper
1/4 cup diced celery
3 tablespoons Garlic Infused Olive Oil
1 tablespoon finely minced garlic
1/3 cup lemon juice, divided
2 tablespoon lemon zest, divided
1 teaspoon thyme leaves
1 tablespoon snipped chives
1 tablespoon Celtic sea salt, divided
1/4 teaspoon cayenne pepper
1/4 teaspoon smoked paprika

Trim tough ends and outer leaves from artichokes. Quarter and quickly brush all cut edges with lemon juice to prevent browning.

In a large heavy bottomed skillet over medium heat sauté celery, red pepper, and garlic in oil until they begin to soften, push aside and add artichokes and brown slightly. Add lemon juice, 1 tablespoon lemon zest, thyme, salt and cayenne. Toss to incorporate and continue cooking until artichokes are tender, add chives.

Divide grits into serving size portions (I use soup plates), top with artichokes and pan juices. Garnish with a sprinkling of lemon zest, paprika and a few fresh chives.

Crab Cakes

No bread crumbs, simply delicious crab and a few grated veggies, herbs and spices give these sumptuous crab cakes a bit of an Asian flair. They are reminiscent of some I had at Wayfarer's restaurant on Cannon Beach.   Despite the long list of ingredients, they come together very quickly. These are so delicious that they need no sauce to embelish the flavor but they also taste fantastic with any Asian inspired sauce.

Yield – 6 medium or 12 small crab cakes

1 teaspoon Wasabi Mayo
1/4 teaspoon San J GF low sodium tamari
1/4 teaspoon Gingery Coconut or Rice Wine Vinegar
1/4 teaspoon Chili-Garlic Oil
1/8 teaspoon toasted sesame oil
1 tablespoon thinly sliced scallions
1 teaspoon chopped cilantro
1 egg lightly beaten
1/8 teaspoon celery seeds
1/8 teaspoon red chili flakes
1 tablespoon finely grated carrots
1 tablespoon finely grated zucchini
1 cup crab meat
1 tablespoon Very Garlic Olive Oil
2 teaspoons peanut oil

Add all ingredients to a medium sized bowl and mix well to ensure egg is equally distributed. Since it is the "glue" that holds these crab cakes together this is a very important step.

Pat into 12 rounds and sauté until golden brown in the combined oils. Drain briefly on toweling then plate on a warm serving platter. Garnish with a few cilantro sprigs.

Summer Vegetable Tartlets

These pretty mini tarts are at perfect for lunch, dinner, brunch or even a cocktail party. Take advantage of zucchini or yellow squash and colorful, sweet, cherry tomatoes at their seasonal peak. Roasting briefly brings out all of the bright flavors while capturing the beautiful colors of these veggies.

Yield – 6 tartelettes

6 unbaked 5 inch Buttery Tart Shells
1 cup Ricotta Substitute
1 1/2 teaspoons nutritional yeast
1/8 teaspoon Celtic sea salt
1/4 teaspoon freshly ground black pepper
1/2 teaspoon Garlic Paste
2 eggs
1 1/4 ounce grated pecorino (about 1 cup)
1 ball Buffo mozzarella cut into 6 slices
1 ounce grated Romano
1 pint cherry tomatoes halved
2 small zucchini
1 teaspoon Basil Infused Olive Oil
1/4 cup torn basil leaves

Preheat oven to 425 degrees. Using a mandoline or a very sharp knife, slice zucchini or yellow squash very thinly and sprinkle liberally with Celtic sea salt. Place in colander over a bowl to drain for about 30 minutes. Just before using, rinse and pat dry.

Arrange tomato halves on a baking sheet. Lightly spray with basil oil and bake 5 minutes. Add squash to pan, spray lightly and bake 5 more minutes, watching carefully since the thin slices of squash can burn easily.

In a medium sized mixing bowl, beat eggs until thick and yellow, add salt, pepper, garlic, nutritional yeast and Ricotta Substitute and beat until light. Divide evenly between unbaked shells and top with a few pieces of torn basil and the other cheeses. Starting with the outside ring, alternating a roasted tomato then 2 thin slices of squash, tomato, squash, etc. in a circle around the outside of the tart. The center should have room for 3 tomatoes and 6 slices of squash. Spray lightly with Basil Oil.

Place tartelettes on a baking sheet in oven, reduce temperature to 375 and bake about 20 minutes or until crust is golden brown and center of tart is set. Cool slightly then remove the tart pan. Sprinkle with additional basil leaves and a sprig of thyme. Serve whole tart as an entrée course or cut into 4 - 6 wedges and serve either warm or room temperature as an appetizer.

Herbed Halibut Wrapped in Parchment Paper

If there is an easier and more delicious way to prepare this firm fleshed fish, I'd be surprised . . . plus this preparation doesn't even require any clean up! Remember this cold water fish is loaded with Omega 3 fatty acids that will do your heart good!
Serves 2

2 4 ounce halibut fillets
1 tablespoon roughly chopped Italian parsley
1 teaspoon thyme leaves
1/2 teaspoon lemon zest
2 tablespoons lemon juice
1/4 teaspoon Tuscan Salt Blend
1/4 teaspoon freshly ground black pepper

Preheat oven to 350 degrees.

Place fish in the center of a 18 inch long piece of unbleached parchment paper. Top fillets with herbs, zest and lemon juice. Fold paper and crease into a pouch and place on a baking sheet.

Bake approximately 8 minutes. Remove from oven, let it rest about 5 minutes. Place on a serving plate and cut the parchment paper and pull back to reveal your beautiful fish.

Breakfast, Brunch and Eggs

Growing up on a farm I learned that breakfast really was the most important meal of the day, and later my medical studies revealed the reason. Eating within the first 45 minutes after awakening resets your body from burning simple carbohydrates during your sleep to using fat stores for greater energy production.

However, the early days of my WF, SF and DF lifestyle left me wondering what to eat! A few months of trial and error later, I emerged with a newfound love for breakfast foods! From delicious hot cereals to GF waffles and pancakes to delicious egg creations, this section will make you a breakfast connoisseur!

My excitement led me to begin entertaining with economical and delicious weekend brunches. My friends and neighbors enjoyed these simple, homey and sometimes elegant meals as much as I did.

And over time I resurrected (with a few twists) some of my favorite lunches and dinners that starred eggs! Using eggs or scrambled tofu as the star of your meal is a quick, economical and very delicious way to have an amazing meal on the table in only minutes!

Check out your local farmer's market for sources of fresh, local, organic eggs and make one of these delicious meals in mere minutes!

Updated Deviled Eggs

As a child in the 1950's deviled eggs were a staple at every party or family get together . . . but then we did have our own chickens. It seems these gems have made a resurgence on the party scene, so I've updated them a little so they literally pop in your mouth! Below are some variations that you can use to add even a little more flavor. They start with this basic recipe then add on layers of flavor. These tasty jewels can also become a main course when combined with a beautiful salad or some steamed veggies.
Yield – 24

12 eggs
4 tablespoons Lemonnaise
2 tablespoon Crème Fraîche Substitute
1 1/2 teaspoon lemon juice
1/2 teaspoon Celtic sea salt
1/4 teaspoon black pepper

Place eggs in a pot large enough so they are not crowded. Fill with enough cold water to cover plus 1 inch. Bring to a slow boil over medium-high heat, boil 3 minutes, cover and turn heat off but leave undisturbed on the burner for 12-15 minutes. Plunge into iced water to cool. Peel and cut eggs in half.

Place yolks in VitaMix or food processor, add remaining ingredients and process until light and smooth. This will give them an airy mousse-like texture.

Rather than using my piping bag, I use a plastic zipper bag when working with egg salad. Simply snip off a corner and insert a tip. Fill bag and pipe into egg whites. However, I also like to use a very large star tip, it's faster, and the result is quite pretty.

Garnish with a dusting of paprika.

NOTE: You can divide your yolk mixture in half and choose the add ins from the recipes below to give you a bit of variety. Choosing a sharp color or flavor contrast will save you time and keep things interesting!

Southwestern Deviled Eggs

These have a bit of a kick from a mix of chilies, which also gives them a beautiful brick-red hue.

For 6 whole eggs briskly stir in the following ingredients:
1/8 teaspoon chipotle powder
1 pinch cayenne pepper
1/8 teaspoon chili powder
1/8 teaspoon smoked paprika
1 pinch cumin
Garnish with coarsely chopped cilantro and a sprinkle of chili powder

Roasted Red Pepper Deviled Eggs

These are smoky, slightly sweet and a beautiful red color. They are one of my personal favorites!

For 6 whole eggs blend the following ingredients into the yolks:
3 tablespoons chopped roasted red peppers
1/8 teaspoon cumin
1/8 teaspoon smoked paprika
Garnish with a piece of roasted red pepper and a sprinkle of paprika

Double-Dilled Deviled Eggs

I love dill pickles and I think they were made to go with eggs. So this version gets a bit of tangy dill pickle relish and some beautiful fresh dill.

For 6 whole eggs blend in the following until mixture is smooth:
2 tablespoons dill pickle relish (or finely chopped dill pickle)
1 teaspoon chopped fresh dill
Garnish with a sprig of fresh dill

Sundried Tomato and Horseradish Deviled Eggs

I love the spicy kick from the horseradish in these eggs . . . a little like a bloody Mary in an egg.

For 6 whole eggs blend in the following until completely smooth:
1/4 teaspoon celery seeds
2 sundried tomatoes packed in olive oil
3/4 teaspoon horseradish
Garnish with a small piece of sundried tomato blotted to remove any excess oil and a sprinkle of paprika

Wasabi Deviled Eggs

Like horseradish, wasabi provides an interesting kick to these eggs. The green wasabi paste as well as the fresh spinach leaves and cilantro produce a pretty green filling.

For 6 whole eggs blend in the following until completely smooth:
2 baby spinach leaves, chopped
1/4 teaspoon wasabi paste
1 teaspoon fresh cilantro chopped
1 dash San-J wheat free, low sodium tamari
Garnish with a few chopped cilantro leaves

Smoked Salmon, Crème Cheese and Caper Deviled Eggs

These fancy Deviled Eggs hold a special surprise and remind me of a great NYC deli! Be sure to process the extra ingredients with the yolks in the VitaMix or food processor to produce a mousse like consistency. Top with a piece of rolled salmon and dill sprigs.

1 tablespoon finely chopped fresh dill
2 tablespoons Ricotta Substitute
1 rounded teaspoon capers
1/4 cup finely chopped smoked salmon
12 sprigs dill as garnish

24 capers for garnish
12 small pieces rolled smoked salmon for garnish

Crab and Wasabi Deviled Eggs

These little devils are a take off on Crab Eggs Benedict. They are so delicious and the surprise of crab and the little kick from wasabi make these a true crowd pleaser! Be sure to process the extra ingredients with the yolks in the VitaMix or food processor to produce a mousse like consistency. Top with a tiny piece of crab and snipped chives or scallions.

1/2 teaspoon wasabi paste
1/4 cup finely minced crab meat
1 rounded teaspoon scallions finely minced
1 teaspoon wheat free tamari
1/4 teaspoon Ginger Paste
1/4 teaspoon red chili flakes
Snipped chives as garnish

Perfect Poached Eggs

I prefer to use egg poaching cups to a vinegar-water bath. They are simple, easy and the egg always turns out perfectly with no "vinegar" taste. Using a silicone cup or a metal poacher takes all of the drudgery and excess water out of the equation, leaving you with a perfect egg every time.
Yield – 4 eggs

4 poaching cups
Olive oil spray
Boiling water
4 whole eggs
Celtic sea salt and black pepper to taste

Very lightly spray egg poaching cups, carefully break eggs and place 1 egg in each cup, float them in boiling water in a covered pot or deep skillet. Sprinkle with salt and pepper. Cover and cook to desired doneness.

 # Tasty Tofu Scramble

The first tofu scramble I ever tried was a mass of spongy, tasteless bits of warm tofu, and I found it absolutely disgusting! However, when marinated and cooked correctly, it is delicious and has both the taste and texture of cheesy scrambled eggs! So for those of you who are either allergic to eggs or are vegan, try this one, I think you will like it.
Serves 4

1 block organic firm tofu drained and lightly pressed
3/4 cup diced yellow onions
3/4 cup julienned Roasted Yellow Pepper
1 tablespoon Spicy Southwestern Olive Oil

Marinade

1 tablespoon Herb Infused Olive Oil
1/2 teaspoon cumin
1 teaspoon grated fresh turmeric or 1/2 teaspoon powdered
3 tablespoons nutritional yeast
1 teaspoon garlic paste
1/2 teaspoon Tuscan Salt Blend
1/2 teaspoon freshly ground black pepper
1/4 teaspoon Italian seasoning
1 pinch red chili flakes

Using a fork break tofu into 1/2 inch sized chunks.
Place tofu, onions and peppers in a bowl with a lid.
In a small bowl combine all marinade ingredients, adding up to a tablespoon of water if necessary to achieve a paste.

Toss marinade with tofu, onions and peppers until well coated. Cover and marinate overnight. If any water accumulates at the bottom of the bowl drain well in a colander set over a bowl.

In a medium sized, heavy bottomed skillet heat oil over medium-high heat. Add tofu and veggie mix and cook until tofu and veggies are warmed through and begin to turn a light golden brown. Should any watery liquid begin to accumulate in the skillet turn up the heat to evaporate. That water will prevent the caramelization of the tofu and veggies, resulting in a rather limp and unappealing scramble. Using a thin metal spatula, turn and cook until lightly golden on the other side.

Serve on a warmed serving platter or individual plates with biscuits, Sweet Potato Hash with Pepitas, or stuffed inside a tortilla with a little salsa.

Sweet Potato Hash with Wilted Spinach and Poached Eggs

This combo is one of the most delicious things I've ever eaten . . . and the colors are so inviting! The sweet potatoes are soft, yet crisp, and their sweetness is a perfect way to balance the slight bitterness of the spinach . . . add to that the creamy softness of the egg yolk . . . words are simply inadequate!
Serves 4

1 recipe Sweet Potato Hash with Pepitas
10 cups fresh spinach tough stems removed
1/4 cup pH 9.5 ionized water
1/2 teaspoon Tuscan Salt Blend
1/2 teaspoon black pepper
1 large pinch red chili flakes
1/2 teaspoon olive oil
4 Perfect Poached Eggs
Olive oil spray

Lightly steam spinach in water, oil, salt, pepper and chili flakes while poaching eggs.

To assemble, divide wilted spinach between 4 plates, top with a layer of hash and a poached egg.

Nutritional Info: This is one of the most nutrient dense dishes you will ever serve! Yams are rich in beta carotene and fiber, while spinach contains exceptionally high levels of bioavailable calcium, pepitas contain very high levels of trace minerals and eggs are rich in sulfur and protein. Together this is combo fights inflammation, boosts the immune system, builds muscles and bones, protectss the nerves and the prostate while feeding the brain!

Sweet Potato Hash with Wilted Spinach and Tasty Tofu Scramble

This combo is one of the most delicious things I've ever eaten . . . and the colors are so inviting! The sweet potatoes are soft, yet crisp, and their sweetness is a perfect way to balance the slight bitterness of the spinach . . . add to that the crisp, yet creamy textures of the tofu scramble and you will be in breakfast, lunch or dinner heaven!
Serves 4

1 recipe Sweet Potato Hash with Pepitas
10 cups fresh spinach with tough stems removed
1/4 cup pH 9.5 ionized water
1/2 teaspoon Tuscan Salt Blend
1/2 teaspoon black pepper
1 large pinch red chili flakes
1/2 teaspoon olive oil
1 recipe Tasty Tofu Scramble

Lightly steam spinach in water, oil, salt, pepper and chili flakes while poaching eggs.

To assemble, divide hash among 4 plates, top with a layer of wilted spinach and a serving of Tasty Tofu Scramble.

 # Very Veggie Frittata

I love the versatility of a frittata!   A simple, yet elegant cousin of the omelet and the quiche it is equally delicious but requires much less time and effort to create. This one has tons of veggies and is packed with flavor. Use your mandolin to make fast work of slicing and it will be ready in a snap! Prep your veggies the night before and your frittata can bake while you get ready for the morning, or serve as a simple, yet elegant brunch or light supper with a salad.
Serves 4-6

1 tablespoon olive oil
1 tablespoon butter
1 med red or white potato
1/2 small red onion
1/2 med zucchini
1/2 med yellow squash
1 1/2 cups baby spinach leaves

4 cloves Roasted Garlic
1/4 julienned red pepper
6 asparagus spears
4 sprigs thyme
1/2 teaspoon fresh rosemary
3 tablespoons chopped Italian parsley
1 sundried tomato
2 tablespoons crumbled feta Cheese
2 tablespoons crumbled goat cheese
6 eggs
Sea salt and black pepper to taste

Preheat broiler.

Using a mandolin or very sharp knife, very thinly slice potatoes, onion, zucchini and yellow squash. Julienne the red pepper. Finely chop garlic and sundried tomato. Remove woody ends from asparagus and slice on the diagonal into 1½ inch pieces.

In a heavy bottomed, ovenproof skillet with a tightly fitting lid, place oil and butter over medium heat. When butter has melted and skillet is warm, begin layering your veggies. First, layer the potatoes followed by the onion slices, half of the herbs, garlic and salt and pepper. Add 2 tablespoons pH 9.5 water and cover skillet. Cook 4 minutes, or until water has evaporated. Follow by layering zucchini, spinach and yellow squash, top with red pepper, asparagus, tomato, cheese, remaining herbs, salt and pepper. Add 1 tablespoon water cover and cook 2-3 minutes to completely heat all veggies.

Lightly beat eggs, add a pinch of salt and pepper and pour over veggies. With a heatproof spatula lift the layered veggies to allow some of the eggs to run under the veggies. Cover and cook until the eggs are set about ½ inch around the sides of the skillet. Uncover and place under broiler until eggs are set.

Your frittata can be served hot straight out of the oven or cooled to room temperature. It serves 4 for breakfast or 6 for lunch or a light supper when served with a salad and bread. Serve your lovely frittata at your next picnic or cut into small wedges to serve as an hors d'oeuvers at your next cocktail party.

Potato Wedges, Spinach and Eggs*

Ever had one of those times when unexpected company dropped by and you had nothing to prepare? Here is something I put together in 20 minutes that will impress your guest. Serve it as a very hearty breakfast, a lovely brunch or a late supper dish with no planning. I used boiled potatoes I had in the refrigerator, but you could substitute Alexis brand potato wedges from the freezer.

Serves 2

2-3 medium sized boiled red potatoes cut into wedges
1 teaspoon butter
1/3 cup diced red onion
1/3 cup diced red pepper
1 teaspoon chopped rosemary
1 sprig thyme, leaves only
3 cups baby spinach
2 eggs
Celtic sea salt and cracked black pepper
2 tablespoons pH 9.5 ionized water

Preheat the oven to 425 degrees.

Place your potato wedges on a baking sheet and spray with olive oil, sprinkle with a pinch of salt and pepper. Bake about 15 minutes then add herbs, turn off oven and the heat will finish the potatoes. They should be crispy, golden brown and smell delicious.

Meanwhile, add butter to a medium sauté pan with a lid. Sauté the onions and peppers until translucent, sprinkle with a small pinch of salt and pepper. Add spinach and stir to combine. Redistribute veggies to make nests for the eggs. Crack an egg into each of the 2 nests and sprinkle with a small pinch of salt and pepper. Add water, cover and steam until spinach is wilted and eggs whites are firm.

Make a nest with the potatoes on each serving plate, place the spinach and egg in the center. Serve immediately.

Cheesy Grits, Garlicky Greens and Poached Eggs*

Whether you are serving this for a hearty and nutritious breakfast, a special brunch or a simple light supper, this is a great way to impress your family and friends in about 10 minutes!
Serves 4

1 recipe Cheesy "Grits"
1 tablespoon butter
3-4 large garlic cloves, sliced thinly
8 - 10 cups baby spinach
2 tablespoons pH 9.5 ionized water
4 Perfectly Poached Eggs
Sea salt and cracked black pepper to taste

Thinly slice garlic – I prefer using a mandolin for even slices – and sauté in butter over medium heat until they are golden and crisp.

Take care that the slices do not over brown or they will become bitter.

Remove from pan with a slotted spoon and drain. To the skillet add water and spinach. Sauté until bright green and somewhat wilted.

In the meantime break eggs into lightly buttered poaching cups. Place cups in pan or skillet that has about 1/2 inch of boiling water, cover and allow to steam until whites are set and yolks are soft, about 4-6 minutes. I prefer to salt and pepper before steaming, but you can omit this if you like.

In the bottom of a shallow bowl spoon in 1 cup of Cheesy "Grits" leaving a well in the center. Top with wilted spinach, a poached egg and some garlic crisps.

*"Veganize" both dishes with 2 simple substitutions! Switch out the Perfect Poached Eggs with Tasty Tofu Scramble and Cheesy "Grits" with Cheezy "Grits".

Perfect Scrambled Eggs

The secret to fluffy scrambled eggs is cook over medium low heat a bit before stirring. This allows the eggs to puff up a bit. Stirring too soon breaks up the eggs into very small pieces and never allows the eggs to reach that "puffy" stage. Gently stir with a wide rubber spatula to break up slightly, allow to cook a bit more, then stir again. Continue until cooked through. Serve immediately.

Egg and Veggie Scramble #1

When you are short on time and still want all the taste of an omlette, this is a quick solution! Filled with sulfur rich eggs and veggies this is a perfect protein building breakfast served alone or a great lunch or light dinner when served over a bed of spinach.
Serves 2

2 teaspoons olive oil or ghee
3 organic eggs
2 tablespoons chopped red onions
2 teaspoons chopped garlic
1/2 cup kale ribbons
2 tablespoons ph 9.5 ionized water
1/4 cup chopped broccoli
1/4 cup grated zucchini
1/4 teaspoons Italian seasoning
1/4 teaspoons each Celtic sea salt and pepper
1/4 cup roughly chopped tomatoes or
2 tablespoons chopped sundried tomatoes

Warm a heavy bottomed sauté pan over medium heat. Add oil or ghee, onions, garlic and seasonings and cook until lightly browned, stirring occasionally.

Meanwhile beat eggs until yolks and whites are incorporated, set aside.

Add water, kale and broccoli, cover and steam/sautéé for about 3 minutes, stirring occasionally. Add zucchini and tomatoes and 1 tablespoon additional water if using sundried tomatoes. Continue to toss veggies for about 30 seconds then add beaten eggs.

When serving over spinach, use baby spinach that has been tossed in a light dressing of 2 teaspoons Tomato Infused Olive Oil and 1/2 teaspoons whole grain country style Mustard and a pinch of salt and pepper.

Egg and Veggie Scramble #2

Here is another quick solution to a flavorful omelet! Filled with sulfur rich eggs and veggies this is a perfect protein building breakfast, or serve over a bed of chopped hearts of Romaine for a light lunch or dinner.
Serves 2

2 teaspoons olive oil or organic ghee
3 organic eggs
2 tablespoons chopped red onions
2 teaspoons chopped garlic
1/2 cup Swiss chard ribbons
2 tablespoons pH 9.5 ionized water
1/2 cup asparagus sliced into 1/4 inch pieces
1/4 cup julienned yellow squash
1/4 teaspoons Italian seasoning
1/4 teaspoons each Celtic sea salt and pepper
1/4 cup Muir Glen diced tomatoes and basil

Warm a heavy bottomed sauté pan over medium heat. Add oil or ghee, onions, garlic and seasonings and cook until lightly browned, stirring occasionally. Meanwhile beat eggs until yolks and whites are incorporated, set aside. Add water, chard and asparagus, cover and steam/sauté for about 3 minutes, stirring occasionally. Add yellow squash and tomatoes and return to a simmer. Continue to simmer until all liquid is absorbed then add beaten eggs.

When serving over hearts of romaine, toss with a light dressing of 2 teaspoons Basil Infused Olive Oil, 2 tablespoons Tomatoes and Basil Vinegar and 1/4 teaspoon salt and pepper.

GF Crème Brulee French Toast

Whole Foods actually serve a delicious dairy laden, wheat bread variety, so I decided that creating a GF and DF version simply had to be done! This recipe is a perfect combo with a crispy top layer, and 2 more layers of soft custard style bread swirled with cinnamon, raisins and maple syrup. It can be assembled the night before and baked the following morning. It makes a beautiful and delicious breakfast or brunch dish and is so simple that kids can make it as a surprise Mother's Day breakfast!
Serves 6-8

1 loaf sliced Rice Bread
3 cups Unsweetened Almond Milk
2 tablespoons Orange Cinnamon Compound Butter
1 teaspoons cinnamon
1/2 teaspoons Sweet Fall Spice Blend
6 organic eggs
1/2 teaspoons stevia
1/4 teaspoons Celtic sea salt
1/4 cup organic raisins
1/3 cup coarsely chopped walnuts
1/3 cup grade "B" maple syrup
2 teaspoons ground flax seeds

Butter a 6 x 9 inch baking dish and set aside. Lightly butter each side of the bread slices. In a bowl, beat the eggs, almond milk, spices, maple syrup, stevia and salt until frothy.

Space bread slices in a single layer in the baking dish, cutting if necessary to fit. Top layer with 1/3 of the walnuts, 1/3 of the raisins and 1 teaspoons ground flax seeds. Repeat 2 more times so that you have 3 layers of sliced bread, nuts and raisins. Pour egg mixture evenly over all of the bread. Push bread down to ensure all slices are saturated. Cover and refrigerate for at least 20 minutes and refrigerating overnight works great. Preheat the oven to 350°. Place baking dish in the center of the oven and bake until a knife inserted in the center comes out clean, about 45 minutes.

Remove from oven, allow to rest for about 10 minutes, and serve with warm maple syrup. Cut any leftovers into 1-2 inch cubes and serve cold as a yummy bread pudding style dessert with just a drizzle of maple syrup and a dusting of powdered sugar

GF Waffles and Pancakes 101

To be perfectly honest, when it comes to GF pancakes and waffles I prefer using a mix – Namaste's Pancake and Waffle Mix – as the base.   This mix is quick, requires fewer ingredients and turns out reliably every time. With a few substitutions and additions you can make a light, crisp waffles or tender pancakes that taste delicious.   Remember to freeze any extras you may make for a quick breakfast on a busy morning! In addition to the recipe for plain batter, on subsequent pages you will find a few of my favorite varieties . . .

Yield – 4 Belgian waffles or 8 4 inch pancakes

1 cup Namaste GF Waffle and Pancake Mix
1 egg separated (or egg replacer)
1 tablespoon walnut oil
1/3 cup almond milk
1 tablespoon yogurt
2 teaspoons flax meal

Beat egg white to stiff peak stage – this will add a lot of "lift" to the batter, resulting in a lighter waffle, this step is unnecessary if making pancakes. Set aside.

Triple sift the mix and flax meal – this makes the flour lighter which results in a waffle or pancake with a lighter texture.

Beat egg yolk, or egg replacer, oil, almond milk and yogurt until light and add to flour. Whisk until blended then gently fold in egg whites.

Pour batter on hot waffle iron and bake. These waffles bake a little faster so watch carefully. If making pancakes, heat griddle until a drop of batter bubbles up and browns evenly. Lightly oil a paper towel and wipe over griddle between batches.Add your favorite toppings and enjoy.

Nutrition Tip: Using Grade "B" Organic Maple Syrup adds more than delicious sweet flavor to your pancakes or waffles! It is also a nutrient dense sweetener containing Vitamin B's, Omega 6 fatty acids, and even calcium, iron, magnesium, copper and potassium. Most importantly, 2 tablespoons of Grade "B" maple syrup contains more than 50% of your recommended amount of manganese and 25% of your recommended amount of zinc. Together these minerals protect your blood vessels, boost your immune system and increase levels of SOD - the super antioxidant aka superoxide dismutase!

GF Blueberry Waffles with Fresh Blueberry Syrup

These are wonderful and can be made with fresh or frozen berries. Just make these simple changes:

Replace plain yogurt for blueberry yogurt
Add 1/2 cup blueberries and 1 teaspoon lemon zest

To serve, cut waffles into sections (or stack pancakes), and arrange on individual plates, top with blueberry yogurt and fresh blueberries, then drizzle with fresh blueberry syrup and a sprinkle of lemon zest.

Using the same method choose your favorite yogurt-berry combos.

PB&B Pancakes

For most of my life I have eaten peanut butter and banana sandwiches with a small drizzle of honey and for most of my life I have eaten peanut butter on my pancakes and waffles. In more recent years I've traded almond butter for peanut butter but that only seems to have improved the entire concept! Here's one of my favorites . . .

Change oil to match the nut butter you plan to use – peanut oil with peanut butter, almond oil with almond butter, etc. Place half the batter on the griddle or waffle iron then a few thin slices of banana, a few chopped nuts and top with the remaining batter.

To serve, spread with nut butter, add a few more banana slices and a drizzle of honey or maple syrup.

GF Pumpkin & Toasted Walnut Waffles with Maple Crème Fraiche

OK, I need to qualify this point, I actually use baked yam puree, not pumpkin in these waffles. I like the flavor better, but feel free to use pumpkin if you like. These tender, crisp waffles are slightly sweet from the yams, nicely spiced and are the perfect way to bring the feeling of fall to your breakfast table any time of year! I use Old Chatham's sheep's milk maple yogurt as the base for the Maple Crème Fraiche Substitute, but you can accomplish the same thing by adding a bit of maple syrup to your favorite yogurt and following the same instructions.

Yield 4 Belgian waffles

1 cup Namaste GF Waffle and Pancake Mix
1 egg separated (or egg replacer)
1 tablespoon toasted walnut oil
1/2 cup almond milk
3 tablespoons yam puree or pureed pumpkin
1/2 teaspoon Fall Spice Blend
2 tablespoons chopped roasted walnuts
1 tablespoon flax meal

Beat egg white to stiff peak stage – this will add a lot of "lift" to the batter, resulting in a lighter waffle. Set aside. (Omit this step if using egg replacer)

Triple sift the mix, spices and flax meal – this makes the flour lighter which results in a waffle with a lighter texture. Add toasted walnuts and mix to combine. This step keeps the walnuts equally distributed in the batter so they don't all drop to the bottom.

Beat egg yolk, or egg replacer, oil, almond milk and puree until light and add to flour. Whisk until blended then gently fold in egg whites.

Pour batter on hot waffle iron and bake. This batter is slightly dense so they take a bit longer to bake.
To serve, arrange on individual plates, top with a dollop of Maple Crème Fraiche Substitute, a sprinkling of roasted walnuts and a drizzle of warm maple syrup.

Raspberry-Thyme Waffles with Lemon Crème and Fresh Raspberry-Thyme Syrup

There is just something perfect about raspberries and lemon, which makes thyme a perfect herb to use. Thyme is slightly lemony in flavor and is delicate as are raspberries. Topped with smooth Lemon Crème and ruby colored, sweet and tart fresh syrup . . . it is so very yummy!

Yield - 4 Belgian Waffles

To the basic GF Waffle recipe make the following changes:

Substitute raspberry yogurt

Add 1/2 cup fresh or 1/4 cup frozen raspberries (do not defrost)

1/2 teaspoon lemon zest

1 tablespoon lemon juice

1/2 teaspoon thyme leaves

To make the Lemon Crème, combine equal parts Lemon Curd and Crème Fraiche Substitute.

To serve, arrange waffles on plates, top each waffle with 1 tablespoon Lemon Crème, then top with fresh syrup, including berries, and a small sprig of thyme.

Fresh Blueberry Syrup

This is a dark purple, super flavorful, syrup that's not too sweet. Using frozen berries is best, because they give up their delicious juice so willingly. So this one is quick to make by simply creating a puree of blueberries. Make it at the last minute because blueberries contain a lot of pectin so it can become rather gelatinous when broken down this way.

Yield – 1 cup

1 1/4 cups frozen blueberries

3 tablespoons fresh lemon juice

2 tablespoons raw honey or agave nectar

1 pinch stevia powder

1 teaspoon lemon zest

Puree defrosted blueberries, lemon juice, honey or agave nectar and stevia powder until smooth in VitaMix or other powerful blender, adding water if necessary. Zest lemon using a medium microplane or zester then fold into puree.

Fresh Raspberry-Thyme Syrup

Is there anything more beautiful than the ruby colored juice from raspberries? This fresh syrup maintains all of the beneficial enzymes, vitamins and minerals of the fresh berries, so it not only tastes amazing it's also amazingly nutritious! The blend of flavors in this fresh syrup will make you look for ways to use it!
Yield – 1 cup

1 cup frozen raspberries, defrosted
1 cup fresh raspberries
2 tablespoons fresh lemon juice
1/2 teaspoon lemon zest
2 tablespoons agave nectar
1 small pinch stevia powder
1 teaspoon thyme leaves.

Puree frozen raspberries. I actually like the seeds in this puree, but if you don't you can pass the puree through a mesh strainer to remove all or most of them. Stir in the remaining ingredients. I like to let it sit for at least 15 minutes to allow the thyme, lemon and raspberries to meld.

Fresh Plum Syrup

When I lived in Spokane some elderly neighbors had the most prolific old fashioned plum tree. Each summer I picked and picked and picked plums for them, for my neighbors and of course, for myself. They were so delicious! This creation of fresh plum slices and thick, sweet, syrupy juices was developed to utilize those plums as well as the other beauties that I found at my local organic farmers' market. Use as many varieties as you can find to make this syrup. The visual effect of the deep red, dark purple, bright yellow and orange flesh of the plums is stunning! Make extra and freeze for a treat on a dreary winter day.
Yield – 1 quart

1 1/2 pounds mixed ripe plums
3-4 tablespoons agave nectar
1 small pinch sea salt (red Hawaiian is perfect)
1 sprig thyme
2 tablespoons lemon juice

Over a bowl to catch juices, pit plums and cut into 3/8 inch slices. Sprinkle plums with lemon juice and salt. Depending upon the sweetness of your plums add agave and stir to distribute. "Bury" the thyme sprig among the plums, cover and macerate overnight in the refrigerator. The plums will release a great deal of syrupy goodness. Remove the thyme sprig and serve both slices and syrup over cereal, waffles, pancakes, shortcakes or pound cake.

 ## Coconut Quinoa in Fresh Plum Syrup

This is one of the most delicious, nutritious and beautiful breakfast or brunch dishes you will ever serve. Cooking the quinoa in coconut milk gives it a creamier texture, but the individual grains still have the slight crunch we love about the grain. The Fresh Plum Syrup and the brightly colored plum slices are so gorgeous against the creamy white cereal that it is visually stunning . . . then you take a bite and are instantly taken to cereal heaven! (Photo page 158)
Serves 4

1 cup white quinoa
1 cup pH 9.5 ionized water
1 cup Thai Kitchen organic coconut milk
2 tablespoons agave nectar
1/8 teaspoon salt
1/4 cup Fresh Plum Syrup
24 plum slices
4 teaspoons chopped almonds

Place quinoa in a fine mesh colander and rinse well then soak in pH 9.5 ionized water for about 10 minutes. Drain well and place in a 2 quart sauce pan. Over medium-high heat lightly toast quinoa until dry and fragrant. Add water, salt and 1/2 cup of the coconut milk, cover and bring to a boil. Boil 5 minutes then turn heat off but leave pot in place on hot burner for 15-20 minutes. This will steam the quinoa and it will be perfectly tender and delicious.

To serve divide among bowls, top with remaining coconut milk, 1 tablespoon Fresh Plum Syrup, 6 slices of the plums from the syrup and a teaspoon of chopped almonds.

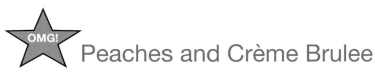

Peaches and Crème Brulee

This is such a great way to start your day! Organic brown rice is so mineral dense . . . and this dish uses both brown rice cereal and brown rice syrup, so it is doubly nutritious. You can use either fresh or frozen peach slices, both are wonderful!
Serves 4

3 cups Very Vanilla or Unsweetened Almond Milk
1 cup farina style creamy brown rice cereal
1/2 teaspoon ground or freshly grated cinnamon
1/4 cup brown rice syrup
Fresh or frozen peach slices
4 teaspoons toasted pistachios
1/4 cup Coconut Whipped Creme

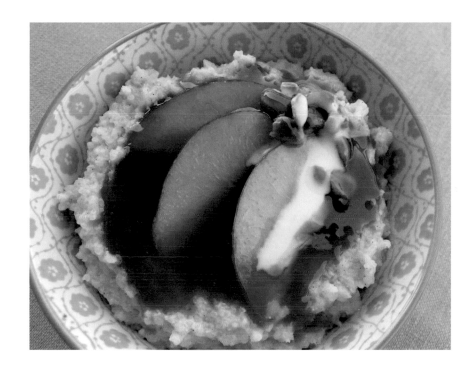

Bring almond milk, cinnamon and 1 tablespoon of the brown rice syrup to a rolling boil. Whisk cereal in slowly, and return to a boil. Reduce heat to simmer, cover and cook, stirring occasionally about 8 minutes.

Prepare the toppings - toast pistachios, cool and roughly chop; slice peaches if using fresh or completely defrost frozen slices.

Heat remaining brown rice syrup in a small saucepan just until it boils. This step should be performed just before serving since the resulting crème caramel can set up quickly.

Divide the creamy cereal in 4 bowls, arrange peaches and pistachios, spoon hot brown rice syrup over and add a dollop of Coconut Whipped Topping. The syrup will set up and turn into a slightly crunchy topping.

Feel free to use a bit of extra coconut milk or topping if desired.

Crispy Peppered Tempeh Bac'n

If you are both WF or GF and meat free the taste of breakfast meats has been impossible to find . . . until now! This is a crisp, meaty, salty, peppery, substitute that is absolutely fantastic. Choose the variety of tempeh you enjoy, keeping in mind that some are WF blends and others are totally GF.
Serves 3-4

1 8 ounce package organic tempeh
3 tablespoons coconut liquid aminos
1 tablespoon WF San J tamari
1 tablespoon grade "B" maple syrup
1 tablespoon juniper berries
1/4 teaspoon garlic granules
1 teaspoon coarse ground black pepper
2 teaspoons Very Garlic Olive Oil

Grind juniper berries in a spice grinder. Mix all liquids and spices until combined.

Slice tempeh as thinly as you can. Place enough slices in a glass refrigerator pan to cover. Pour half of the liquids over and then place remaining slices on top, running in the opposite direction. Pour remaining liquid over, cover and refrigerate overnight turning over to recoat the tops at least twice.

Preheat oven to 250 degrees. Spread oil evenly over a rimmed baking sheet. Lay tempeh out on tray leaving a little space between each piece. Bake 20 minutes turn over, baste with the marinade. Increase the oven temperature to 375 degrees and bake until browned and crisp, about 20 minutes.

Don't be fooled by the dark browning, they are not burned. The sugars from the maple syrup combined with the tamari create a fairly dark appearance that deepens as it crisps.

Country Style Tempeh Breakfast Sausage

This is a wonderful meat-free, WF and GF breakfast sausage alternative! Easy to prepare and surprisingly realistic in color, flavor and texture. I think you will really like this one!
Serves 4

1 8 ounce package organic tempeh
3 tablespoons coconut liquid aminos
1 tablespoon WF San J tamari
1 tablespoon grade "B" maple syrup
1 teaspoon juniper berries
1 teaspoon fennel seeds
1/2 teaspoon cumin seeds
1 teaspoon ground sage
1/4 teaspoon Bruschetta Seasoning Blend
1/4 teaspoon garlic granules
1 teaspoon coarse ground black pepper
1 tablespoon Herb Infused Olive Oil

Lightly toast fennel and cumin seeds, cool slightly then grind with juniper berries. Mix all liquids (except oil) and seasonings together until smooth.

Slice tempeh into 3/8 to 1/2 inch slices and place in a flat bottomed glass dish with a lid. Pour marinade over tempeh and brush to coat all sides. Marinate at least 4 hours, overnight is best.

Place oil in a heavy bottomed skillet over medium heat. Sauté tempeh in oil until browned and crisp around the edges. Serve warm.

Breads, Muffins, Biscuits and Crackers

I love bread! All kinds of bread, from biscuits to muffins to yeast breads. But when I had to give up wheat, I was not too enamored with my options, and I found GF breads down right terrible! Since I could not imagine living the rest of my life without bread, I started experimenting.

In my 1st cookbook I provided basic spelt, garbanzo and brown rice loaves that are delicious, but this time I took on much more complicated recipes. From GF Sourdough Bread to a super easy No-Knead Spelt Ciabatta loaf, from light and fluffy GF biscuits and muffins to some truly tasty crackers, they are not only delicious, each of them also packs a nutritional punch!

Remember baking is chemistry, so get out your measuring cups, preheat your oven and bake some bread you can enjoy!

GF Sourdough Starter

This is an entirely different looking animal than its spelt cousin, but the principles are the same. Because there is no gluten in the flours it does require a bit more frequent feedings. It produces the best bread after 5 days or more and about that same time it can start living in your refrigerator with less frequent feedings.

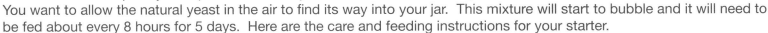

11/2 cup100 degree ph 8.5 ionized water
1/3 cup GF oat flour
1 teaspoon dry organic yeast
1/3 cup sweet brown rice flour or glutinous rice flour
1 teaspoon xanthan or guar gum
1/2 teaspoons black strap molasses

In a wide mouth quart jar or crock mix the dry ingredients together and stir in the water until completely incorporated. Loosely cover to allow air exchange. You want to allow the natural yeast in the air to find its way into your jar. This mixture will start to bubble and it will need to be fed about every 8 hours for 5 days. Here are the care and feeding instructions for your starter.

After 8 hours feed it by stirring in 1/4 cup warm pH 9.5 water with 1/4 teaspoons black strap molasses dissolved in it. Cover and let it bubble away . . .

After 8 more hours mix in 1/4 cup GF oat flour and 1/2 cup warm pH 8.5 water with 1/4 teaspoon black strap molasses.

After 8 more hours remove 3/4 to 1 cup of the starter (use it to make pancakes if you like) and mix in 1/3 cup sweet brown rice flour and 1/2 cup water.

Every 8 hours following this add 1/4 teaspoon black strap molasses in 1/2 cup water and alternate between 1/4 cup oat flour and sweet brown rice flour. Every day or every other day remove up to 1 cup of the starter and use it or toss it.

On the 4th or 5th day you will see a liquid beginning to form that is referred to as hooch. In wheat or spelt starters it smells like beer, but in this GF starter it smells more like rice wine. If you start to have too much hooch when you add the flour do not add any water. This hooch is very important in a GF sourdough starter, because it provides that tangy sour taste. But if there is too much it is an indication that it needs a little more to feed on and that it is time to start living in the refrigerator. The cool temp in the fridge will slow the growth of the yeast down so it will only need to be stirred and fed every day or two. To store it in the refrigerator use a clean wide mouth jar or crock. Feed your starter and pour it into the jar. I use sprouting lids for air circulation but a regular lid slightly ajar will also work. To use refrigerated starter, take it out at least a few hours ahead of your baking, overnight is actually better. Feed it with oat or sweet brown rice flour and a 1/4 teaspoons of black strap molasses, adding water if necessary. When it is bubbling, smelling sour and warm it is ready to go!

You can share your starter with a friend and they will be very grateful. While it is virtually impossible to kill it once it goes into the fridge, it is a great idea to provide care and feeding instructions. Soon you will have many converts. It is somewhat addictive!

Spelt Sourdough Starter

Sourdough is the secret weapon in spelt break baking! Yeast plays a number of important roles in bread making and one of them is this . . . it develops the gluten. This is especially important in non-wheat breads because they are much lower in their gluten content. So using a sourdough starter for all or part of the yeast in your breads will dramatically improve the texture of your breads

1 cup warm ph 8.5 ionized water
1 cup white spelt flour
1 teaspoon organic dry yeast
1/2 teaspoon black strap molasses

In a quart jar mix the water, molasses, flour and yeast until smooth. Cover loosely, store in a 60-80° place in your kitchen and stir twice a day. Every 24 hours remove half of the starter and feed the remainder with 1/2 cup pH 8.5 ionized water and 1/2 cup spelt flour.

Because you are starting with a little yeast your starter will progress more quickly than if you rely solely on wild yeast from the air. Within 2 days (depending upon temperature) you will start seeing a brownish liquid form. This is referred to as hooch and it smells like beer. Stir it back into your starter. When your starter develops a bubbly froth it's complete. Now you can feed it, put it in a clean jar and store it in the refrigerator loosely covered.

Stir your starter a few times a week and feed it about once a week to keep it going. If it ever develops green, orange or black mold throw it away and start over. To use the refrigerated starter, remove it from the refrigerator at least 4 hours (overnight is better) in advance, feed it 1/4 cup white or whole spelt flour and 1/4 cup warm water with 1/4 teaspoons black strap molasses and let it perk up and get bubbly before using it. (Exception—when using in the No-Knead Ciabatta Bread, there is no need to do anything except measure it and mix it in. This is due to the exceptionally long rising time.)

Any spelt bread recipe you are baking can use a little sourdough starter to assist in the gluten development. Please note it does not make more gluten, it simply enhances the structure of the existing gluten which results in a much lighter, airier, more delicious bread. Even sweet breads benefit from a sourdough starter and there are also many wonderful pancake recipes you can try with the early starter rather than throwing it away.

If you feel a bit attached to your starter and don't like throwing it away, you can start a few other jars to give away as gifts. Be sure to provide care and feeding instructions with your gift.

GF Sourdough Bread

I cannot believe I actually pulled this off! It took me 2 attempts and it is absolutely wonderful. I shared it with my neighbors who are not GF and they loved it! It has a crisp outer crust, a moist, spongy texture, and it has a buttery taste with a slight sourdough tang! It requires a very long rise time so you can make the sponge before bed and finish the dough in the morning or mix it up before you leave for work, finish it when you get home and have hot, fresh bread for dinner! Yield 1 loaf or 12 dinner rolls

1/2 cup100 degree ph 8.5 ionized water
4 teaspoons ground flax seeds
3/4 teaspoons dry organic yeast*
1 teaspoon liquid lecithin
2 eggs at room temperature
1/4 cup extra virgin olive oil
3/4 cup GF sourdough starter
1 teaspoon xanthan gum
1 1/2 teaspoons Celtic sea salt
2 cups Bob's Red Mill GF All Purpose Baking Flour
1/2 cup brown rice flour
2-3 tablespoons organic blue cornmeal

In a large warmed mixing bowl add the water and the yeast. Dissolve and allow to sit for 3-5 minutes. Add the eggs, sour-dough starter, ground flax seeds, lecithin, olive oil and Xanthan gum and mix with a paddle attachment on your mixer for 2 minutes. Cover the bowl and set it in draft free place for 8-10 hours. The sponge will rise and become quite bubbly.

Return the bowl to the mixer and with the paddle attachment mix in the salt and the flours 1/2 cup at a time, beating well after each addition until the dough is light and rather fluffy. It will be sticky.

Using a metal loaf pan, or muffin tin oil or butter it well then dust rather heavily with organic blue cornmeal.

Scrape the dough into the pan, level with a spatula and a little olive oil. Cover and set the pan in a warm, draft free area until the dough is level with the top of the pan. Depending upon the warmth of your kitchen, this can take up to 1 1/2 hours.

Preheat your oven to 425°. Place the loaf pan in the center of the oven and bake for 30 minutes. Lower the heat to 350° and con-tinue baking until tester comes out clean, but DO NOT over bake. (This can take up to 45 more minutes depending upon your oven.) Once the temperature has been reduced test after 30 minutes and then every 8 10 minutes after that.

Remove from oven and cool on a rack for about 5 minutes, care-fully remove from the loaf pan and allow to cool on the rack until it is just slightly warm before cutting.

If you can refrain from eating the entire loaf, store it in a plastic zipper bag. It is great when sliced, then immediately frozen in a zipper bag. When you want a slice or 2 of fresh, warm bread, take as many slices as you want out of the bag and wrap in foil, heat in a 350° oven for about 10 minutes or until warm and enjoy!

NOTE: If you are in a humid climate, increase active dry yeast to 2 teaspoons.

No-Knead Spelt Ciabatta Bread

This is the easiest, most delicious bread I have ever made in my entire life! It takes about 4 or 5 minutes to mix it up and a total of 20 hours to rise, so it takes a little thoughtful planning and it is so worth it! Just like traditional ciabatta it is a fairly flat bread, rising only about 2 inches. So you cut the bread into squares, then split in half to make sandwiches.
Yield - 10x12 inch loaf.

3/4 cup 100 degree pH 8.5 ionized water
1 1/2 teaspoons Celtic sea salt
3/4 teaspoon organic dry yeast
2/3 cup Spelt Sourdough Starter
3 cups white spelt flour*
3 cups whole spelt flour*

In a large mixing bowl add the water and the yeast. Dissolve and let it sit for 3-5 minutes. Add the Spelt Sourdough Starter and the flours, stir until well incorporated. This dough will be sticky. Cover it with parchment paper and allow to rise in a 60-65° place for 18 hours. The surface of the dough will be covered with air bubbles at this point. If your kitchen is too warm it will over rise so you will need to move it to a cooler location.

Lightly oil a pan that measures approximately 10 x 12 inches with a 1 inch or higher lip. (The pan I use is an enamel coated pan from an old toaster oven. Metal pans will always produce a better crust than a glass pan.) Sprinkle the pan generously with blue corn meal and set it aside. The lip is necessary for this bread to force it to rise up rather than just out.

With a rubber spatula fold the dough over itself to deflate. Scrape the dough out of the bowl with the spatula on to a well floured surface and flour the top of the dough. Push and pull the sticky dough into the shape of the pan. Now invert the pan on top of the dough and bring the plastic wrap up over the pan. Hold the plastic wrap and the pan firmly and quickly flip it over. Be certain that the top of the dough is well floured. Place a well floured towel to cover and allow to rise for 2 hours.

Preheat the oven to 425°. Place the pan in the center of the oven and bake until the loaf sounds hollow when you tap on it, about 30-40 minutes. Remove from pan and cool on a wire rack until only slightly warm before cutting.

*Spelt flours vary widely in their moisture content. I like VitaSpelt best and find it to be the most reliably consistent.

GF Southern Buttermilk Biscuits

In my first cookbook I shared my recipe for absolutely delicious Spelt Southern Buttermilk Biscuits but still had no GF Version. I had tried, believe me I had tried in fact some of my versions were so horrible that when I turned them into dog biscuits my dogs got stomach aches!   But one morning, I just got inspired and here they are . . . GF biscuits that are very close to my Mom's flaky, tender biscuits, so enjoy them with your favorite toppings like butter and jam or turn them into inspired biscuit sandwiches with veggie scramble, Cauliflower Gravy or Oven Fried Chicken or Tofu!
Yield – 8 2 inch biscuits

1/2 cup + 1 tablespoon GF oat flour
1/2 cup Gluten Free Mama's Almond Blend Flour
1 tablespoon Arrowroot
¼ teaspoon xanthan or guar gum
1 teaspoon each baking powder and ground flax seed
¼ teaspoon each baking soda and sea salt
1/4 cup palm shortening
1/2 cup Buttermilk Substitute
1 teaspoon nutritional yeast

Preheat oven to 425 degrees. In a bowl whisk together all dry ingredients except nutritional yeast. With a pastry cutter blend in shortening until it resembles very course corn meal. Set in freezer for 5-10 minutes to chill thoroughly.

Mix nutritional yeast with your favorite Buttermilk Substitute. I prefer the "whey" from either nut cheese or from draining yogurt. The nutritional yeast adds a "buttery" flavor to the biscuits while maintaining a lighter texture.

Make a well in the center of your dry ingredients and add liquid. Mix with a fork just until a dough begins to come together. Turn out on to a floured board and knead a few times until you have a cohesive, but slightly sticky dough. Humidity and temperature do effect flour, so if yours is a bit dry add additional whey, ½ teaspoon at a time to achieve a slightly sticky dough.

Pat or lightly roll ½ to ¾ inch thick. Cut with a biscuit cutter or sharp knife and place on a baking sheet. Bake in the top 1/3 of your oven for about 10 minutes. The biscuits will be a light golden brown. Do not over bake or they will be dry and crumbly. Serve while hot with your favorite toppings, or slice and make into delicious breakfast sandwiches!

Strawberry and Goat Cheese Muffins with Thyme Leaves

These muffins are tender, slightly sweet with creamy goat cheese nuggets. The mellow thyme leaves add just a hint of savory goodness.

Yield – 12 large muffins

1 1/2 cups organic white spelt flour
1/2 cup organic palm sugar or evaporated cane juice
1 1/2 teaspoon baking powder
1/4 teaspoon baking soda
1/4 teaspoon Celtic sea salt
1/2 teaspoon fresh thyme leaves
3/4 cup goat yogurt
1 egg, slightly beaten
4 tablespoons melted butter
1/4 teaspoon Strawberry Balsamic Vinegar
3/4 cup fresh or defrosted strawberries roughly chopped
2 ounces very coarsely crumbled goat cheese

Preheat oven to 350 degrees. Line muffin tins with papers.

In a mixing bowl whisk together all dry ingredients and thyme leaves make a well in the center and set aside.

In a small bowl whisk together the yogurt, egg and butter. Pour into the well and mix just until incorporated. There will still be lumps. Fold in berries and goat cheese.

With an ice cream scoop or spoon gently scoop batter into muffin cups. Bake in the center of the oven for about 20 minutes or until a tester comes out clean. Cool in pan for about 5 minutes, remove and serve or cool on a rack. When completely cooled, store in an airtight container or wrap well and freeze. If you would like to reheat, place in a parchment paper bag, then foil and reheat about 10 minutes at 300 degrees for frozen muffins and 5 minutes for defrosted muffins.

GF Cranberry Muffins with Goat Cheese and Rosemary Pecans

We can all use a little help now and then . . . and what's faster and easier than calling on the experts who have created mixes we can use as a basic batter and then customize? This version is an interesting combination of tart, tangy and savory flavors. And best of all you know they will turn out perfectly every time!
Yield – 1 dozen

1 Namaste Sugarless Muffin Mix
1/8 teaspoon stevia powder
1 cup fruit sweetened dried cranberries
1/3 cup coarsely chopped Rosemary Pecans
1/2 cup goat's milk yogurt
1/2 cup pH 9.5 ionized water
2 eggs
1/2 cup pecan, or almond oil
2 ounces coarsely crumbled goat cheese
1 tablespoon Vanilla Sugar

Preheat oven to 375 degrees and line muffin tin.

Add muffin mix to a medium mixing bowl. Add pecans and cranberries, whisk, make a well in the center and set aside. In a small bowl beat together eggs, water, yogurt and oil. Pour into well and mix until well combined. Gently fold in goat cheese crumbles.

Divide evenly among 12 paper lined muffin cups. Sprinkle with sugar. Bake about 18 minutes or until a tester inserted in the center comes out clean. Cool slightly before removing from muffin tin and serve hot.

Store leftovers in an airtight container, or wrap in parchment paper then foil and freeze up to 3 months. To reheat, place frozen muffins in a 300 degree oven for 10 minutes, defrosted muffins take only 5 minutes.

# Vegan Zucchini Muffins

Tender, moist and totally yummy . . . these muffins are nicely spiced and studded with crunchy walnuts.
Yield – 9 muffins

1/2 cup whole spelt flour
1/2 cup + 1 tablespoon white spelt flour
1/2 teaspoon ground flax seed
1 teaspoon cinnamon
1 tablespoon baking powder
1/8 teaspoon Celtic sea salt
1/2 cup packed shredded zucchini
3/4 cup almond milk
1/4 cup walnut oil
1/4 cup maple syrup
1/4 cup chopped walnuts

Preheat oven to 350 degrees. Line muffin tins with papers.

In a medium sized mixing bowl, combine all dry ingredients and make a well in the center. In a separate small bowl combine wet ingredients then pour into well.
Whisk until combined without over mixing.

Fill muffin tin 3/4 full. Bake in the center of the oven for approximately 30 minutes.

Raspberry, Orange and Sour Crème Muffins

Yummy, tender and quick to make! These treats are perfect with a cup of tea or your favorite latte any time of the day.
Yield – 1 dozen

1 1/4 cups spelt flour
1 cup raspberries
1/4 cup Sour Crème Substitute
3 tablespoons Orange Curd
2 tablespoons almond oil
1/2 teaspoon baking powder

1/2 teaspoon baking soda
1/4 teaspoon Celtic sea salt
1 egg or egg replacer
2 tablespoons Orange Sugar

In a small bowl whisk together flour, baking powder, soda, salt and half of the Orange Sugar. Add the raspberries and stir to coat with flour mixture. Make a well in the center.

In a separate bowl whisk egg, oil, orange curd and sour crème until well combined. Pour into the well and mix until just combined. Spoon into paper lined muffin cups, sprinkle tops with remaining Orange Sugar and bake about 20 minutes or until toothpick inserted in center comes out clean. Transfer to a wire rack to cool slightly before serving.

GF Raspberry, Orange and Sour Crème Muffins

These turn out just as yummy, and tender as their spelt cousins! And they can be frozen and reheated for a perfect treat anytime! Enjoy with a cup of tea or your favorite latte.
Yield – 8-10 muffins

1 1/2 cups Gluten Free Mama's Almond Blend Flour
1/4 teaspoon guar or xanthan gum
1 cup raspberries
1/4 cup Sour Crème Substitute
3 tablespoons Orange Curd
2 tablespoons almond oil
1/2 teaspoon baking powder
1/2 teaspoon baking soda
1/4 teaspoon Celtic sea salt
1 egg
2 tablespoons Orange Sugar

In a small bowl whisk together flour, baking powder, soda, salt and half of the Orange Sugar. Add the raspberries and stir to coat with flour mixture. Make a well in the center.

In a separate bowl whisk egg, oil, orange curd and sour crème until well combined. Pour into the well and mix until just combined.

Spoon into paper lined muffin cups, sprinkle tops with remaining Orange Sugar and bake about 20 minutes or until toothpick inserted in center comes out clean. Cool on a wire rack in the pan for about 8 minutes before serving.

GF Goat Cheese Crackers

These crackers are a bit like a thin, savory shortbread. They are such wonderful, crackery treats to serve with soups or on a cheese and fruit tray. Super simple to whip up, they are a wonderful substitute for croutons along side a salad. They can be made up to 1 week in advance and stored in an airtight container. (Additional Photo on page 39.)
Yield - 24

1/3 cup GF Pastry Flour Blend or GF Mama's Almond Flour Blend
1/8 teaspoon guar or xanthan gum
1 teaspoon flaxseed meal (ground flaxseeds)
1 teaspoon nutritional yeast
1/4 teaspoon Celtic sea salt
2 tablespoons room temperature butter
1/3 cup room temperature goat cheese, Yogurt Cheese or Cashew Goat Cheeze

Preheat oven to 350 degrees.
Unlike making pastry dough, the butter and soft cheese needs to be fully incorporated so be certain that all your ingredients are room temperature. In the bowl of your food processor blend all ingredients until a ball of dough forms.
Roll dough into a log, wrap in plastic wrap and refrigerate for about 1 hour or up to 5 days.

Slice into 1/8 inch slices and bake on parchment paper 20-25 minutes or until crackers are golden brown. Remove from oven and cool at least 5 minutes before removing parchment paper to a wire rack to finish cooling.

GF Blue Cheese and Thyme Crackers

These are so yummy when they are warm and slightly soft, and even better when they are cooled and crisp. The blue cheese shines through and pair perfectly with Blue Cheese Yogurt Cheese Spread.
Yield – 24

GF Goat Cheese Cracker Dough
1 1/2 teaspoon thyme leaves
2 tablespoons Roquefort cheese

Add to the dough, chill, slice and bake according to the directions above.

GF Roasted Red Pepper and Garlic Goat Cheese Crackers

This variation is beautiful with a swirl of red pepper running through the crackers. They pair well with zesty dips, sharp cheeses and apples slices.
Yield – 24

GF Goat Cheese Cracker Dough
1/4 teaspoon garlic granules
1 tablespoon Roasted Red Pepper finely diced

Smash peppers and garlic into a paste. Pat dough out into a rectangle and spread with paste. Work into a cohesive log, wrap and refrigerate. Follow directions on previous page.

GF Black Pepper and Goat Cheese Crackers

I always loved water crackers with black pepper, so these crackers are my homage. These are great with any style cheese as well as a variety of dips.
Yield – 24

GF Goat Cheese Cracker Dough
1 teaspoon freshly ground coarse black pepper

Swirl into the dough, chill, slice and bake according to the directions on previous page.

DESSERTS

While fresh, seasonal fruit can be a stunning ending to a delicious meal, there are times that my inner Cookie Monster and Chocolate Diva require a more decadent dessert!

From ooey-gooey GF cookies, to buttery shortbreads, moist pound cakes and the best GF German chocolate cake and icing to tarts, pies, cobblers, crumbles, crisps and even gelatos, these recipes will impress even the harshest critics!

So no need to eat WF, DF, GF and SF desserts where you wonder if the packaging would have tasted better than its contents! Nor do you have to settle for GF desserts with the nutritional value of a Twinkie! These delicious desserts are also great sources of antioxidants, vitamins, minerals and even fiber!

Now you can enjoy sweet treats that will leave your inner Cookie Monster and Chocolate Diva in ecstasy!

GF Chocolate Chip Cookies

These are seriously great GF cookies! Crisp around the edges, chewy in the middle, just like my spelt version. I swear, no one will ever guess they are GF! The secret is using GF oats! Who knew it could be so easy! So if you are tired of dry, crumbly, tasteless cookies . . . well here's a recipe for you!

1/2 cup butter or palm shortening
1/2 cup organic dark brown sugar
1 egg or egg replacer
1/2 teaspoon black strap molasses
1/2 teaspoon vanilla
3/4 teaspoon baking soda
1/4 teaspoon celtic sea salt
1 1/3 cup GF oat flour
1 tablespoon ground flax seeds
3/4 cup GF rolled oats
1/2 cup chocolate chips
1/2 cup chopped nuts (optional)

Preheat the oven to 350° In the bowl of a mixer beat the butter or shortening and sugar until light and fluffy. Add the egg, vanilla, salt and soda and beat again until it is very light and fluffy.

Add the oat flour and ground flax then mix until combined. Next add rolled oats, chocolate chips and nuts. Mix until thoroughly combined.

I think these cookies are best a bit bigger than average, so I drop them by tablespoons leaving room for them to spread. (Always make a single test cookie to see how much it spreads and if you need to add any additional flour. If the cookie does not hold together or spreads too much add 1 tablespoon of flour and mix in then try another test cookie. Add an additional tablespoon if necessary.) This dough is slightly softer than its spelt counterpart.

Bake in the center of the oven for about 8-10 minutes. Do not over bake! They should be pretty soft in the center when removed from the oven. Cool on the cookie sheet about 8-10 minutes then remove to a cooling rack to cool completely. Store in an airtight container. Freeze preshaped cookies to bake for an instant warm treat anytime!

GF Double Chocolate Shortbread

If you've been missing a crisp little chocolate cookie, this recipe is for you! This versatile recipe can be used to create a crisp treat, sandwich cookies and even a shortbread pie crust!

2 cups GF Mama's Almond Flour Blend
1/2 teaspoon xanthan or guar gum
1/3 cup Tropical Source chocolate chips
Pinch Celtic sea salt
1 cup softened butter or coconut oil
1 cup Superfine Vanilla Sugar OR 2/3 cup cane sugar plus ¼ tsp stevia
3/4 cup unsweetened cocoa powder or raw cacao powder

In a bowl, sift or whisk together the flour, xanthan gum and salt (if using coconut oil increase salt to ½ teaspoon). This is especially important in GF baking to be certain that the Xanthan gum is equally distributed throughout the dough or batter.

In a food processor chop the chocolate chips into pieces approximately equal to ¼ their original size.In the bowl of your electric mixer beat the butter and sugar until light and fluffy about 2 - 3 minutes.   Add the cocoa powder and beat until fully incorporated. Add the dry flour mixture and chocolate chips to the butter, sugar and cacao mixture and beat just until the dough becomes cohesive.

Divide the dough in half. Place each half of dough on a 14 inch length of parchment or wax paper. Shape the dough into a smooth log about 1-2 inches in diameter, depending on the size of cookies you prefer.   Be sure the dough has no air pockets. Thoroughly wrap the shaped logs in the parchment or wax paper, twist the ends of the paper to seal, and refrigerate to chill for at least two hours, or freeze up to 3 months. (If cookie dough is frozen defrost in the refrigerator overnight before continuing.)

Position the oven rack in the center of the oven and preheat to 325 degrees. Line baking sheets with parchment paper. Using a sharp but thin knife, slice the logs into ¼ to 1/2 inch thick rounds. 1/4 inch rounds will produce a crisp cookie and ½ inch will produce a slightly softer cookie. I prefer the thinner cookies when dipping in chocolate and the softer version for making sandwich cookies.

Place the cookies directly on the parchment lined baking sheets, spacing about 2 inches apart to allow for expansion. Bake approximately 10-15 minutes, or until the cookies are beginning to dry and are firm to the touch. Remove from oven, slide parchment paper directly on to a cooling rack and cool completely before handling.

GF Tart Cherry & Pistachio Shortbread Cookies

These are both slightly sweet and savory . . . the pistachio oil adds a roasted nutty flavor and the basil blends so well with tart cherries . . . these must be sampled to be appreciated! Perfect for a cocktail party on your cheese and fruit tray.
Yield – 12-14 cookies

7 tablespoons butter
1 tablespoon pistachio oil
1 cup GF Mama's almond blend flour
2 tablespoons arrowroot
1/2 teaspoon xanthan or guar gum
1/4 cup vanilla sugar
3 tablespoons chopped pistachios
3 tablespoons chopped dried cranberries
1 teaspoon basil in short ribbons

In a small bowl whisk together all dry ingredients.

In the bowl of your electric mixer add butter, oil and sugar. Beat on medium speed until light and fluffy.

Add dry mixture and incorporate on low speed. Add nuts and cranberries and mix until evenly distributed. Now add the basil and fold in by hand.

I like to make mine in 3 small tart pans, however you can pat into a large circle in an 8 inch spring form. Once you have it in your desired pan, cover and refrigerate at least 1 hour.

Bake at 350 degrees until golden brown and somewhat dry, about 15 minutes. Do not over bake.   Remove from oven, cool in pan on a rack about 5 minutes. Cut into wedges with a very sharp serrated knife and then cool completely before handling.

GF Scottish Shortbread Cookies

Scottish shortbread is distinctively tender and nutty from oats and exceptionally buttery. This GF version is no exception! Using date sugar adds another layer of richness to the cookie while boosting its vitamin, mineral and fiber counts!   Great with a scoop of gelato, a cup of tea or in your lunchbox.
Yield – 12-14 wedges

1 cup + 2 tablespoons oat flour
1/2 cup Mama's Gluten Free Almond Flour
1/4 teaspoon guar or xanthan gum
1/2 cup Superfine Palm or Date Sugar*
1 cup room temperature salted butter
1 teaspoon vanilla extract

In a small bowl whisk dry ingredients until fully incorporated. Beat sugar and butter until creamy, add vanilla. Add dry ingredients and mix on low speed just until fully incorporated. Most shortbread is a bit dry, but this dough is a little sticky.

Turn dough out on a baking sheet or tart pan and spread to an even consistency. If using a tart pan, press it up the sides and make it slightly thinner in the center. Cover and refrigerate for at least 1 hour.

Bake at 350 degrees for about 20 minutes. Shortbread should be firm, golden and feel somewhat dry. Remove from oven, dust with a sprinkling of Superfine Palm or Date Sugar and cool completely.

Your scoring lines will still be evident, with a very sharp serrated knife, cut through, remove from tart pan and store in an airtight container.

*Reducing sugar to 2 tablespoons will give you a more cracker style shortbread. These are great with apples, pears and cheese.

My Grandma's Chocolate Drop Cookies – Reinvented

These cookies are more like individual brownie cakes. When I was attempting to find an appropriate cookie for gelato sandwiches I immediately thought of my Grandma's cookies. With very little effort they came out of the oven exactly as I had recalled them from childhood, light and deeply fudgy little cakelike cookies . . . Here they are and I hope you love them as much as I do.
Yield – 36 cookies

1 cup white spelt flour
1/2 teaspoon baking powder
1/4 teaspoon salt
1/4 cup palm shortening
1/3 cup date, palm or cane sugar
1 egg
1/3 cup almond milk
4 tablespoons coco powder dissolved in 4 tablespoons hot water
1 teaspoon vanilla

In a small bowl whisk together the dry ingredients, set aside.

In the bowl of your electric mixer beat shortening and sugar until light a fluffy. Add egg and beat 1 minute. Add almond milk, chocolate and vanilla and beat until fully incorporated. Slowly add flour and mix on medium speed until fully incorporated.

Drop by teaspoonfuls onto a lightly oiled baking sheet and bake in the center of the oven for approximately 7 minutes or until the edges are slightly crisp and the center springs back when touched lightly. Remove from the oven, cool on sheet for 3-5 minutes then transfer to a cooling rack with very small holes until completely cooled. Grandma iced them with butter cream icing, but I generally leave them plain.

My Grandma's Chocolate Drop Cookies – Reinvented and GF

Just like their spelt cousins, these yummy deep chocolate treats were inspired by a cookie my Grandma used to make when I was a little girl. Each bite is moist, fudgy, and a delicious cross between a cookie, a brownie and a cake! They are one of the best GF cookies I've ever developed . . . thanks to my Grandma! Here they are and I hope you love them as much as I do.

Yield – 36 cookies

1 cup Gluten Free Mama's Almond Flour Blend
3/4 teaspoon baking powder
1/4 teaspoon salt
1/4 teaspoon guar or xanthan gum
1/4 cup palm shortening
1/3 cup palm or cane sugar
1 egg
1/3 cup almond milk
4 tablespoons coco powder dissolved in 4 tablespoons hot water
1 teaspoon vanilla

In a small bowl whisk together the dry ingredients, set aside.

In the bowl of your electric mixer beat shortening and sugar until light a fluffy. Add egg and beat 1 minute. Add almond milk, chocolate and vanilla and beat until fully incorporated. Slowly add flour and mix on medium speed until fully incorporated.

Drop by teaspoonfuls onto lightly oiled baking sheets, smooth with the back of a wet spoon and bake in the center of the oven for approximately 7 minutes or until the center springs back when touched lightly. Do not over bake. Remove from the oven, cool on sheet for 3-5 minutes then transfer to a cooling rack with very small holes until completely cooled.

Grandma iced them with buttercream icing, but I generally leave them plain. These cookies make great ice cream sandwiches!

GF German Chocolate Cupcakes

German Chocolate cake was my Dad's and is my daughter Allison's favorite birthday cake. Both were born in March so this cake has been a part of my early spring my whole life. I have tried and tried to make a wheat free version with little success until now! I decided to try start with a surefire cake mix from Namaste and make a few changes . . . the perfect GF German Chocolate cupcake was born! And it could not be easier to make!
Yield - 24

1 Namaste Yellow Cake Mix
4 room temperature eggs, separated or well beaten egg replacer
1 cup ph 9.5 ionized water
1/2 cup coconut oil
1 package of German sweet chocolate

Preheat oven to 350°. In a small pan over low heat melt together the coconut oil and chocolate (break along scored lines for better results) stirring constantly. Set aside to cool slightly.

Place egg whites in a small mixing bowl and beat until they form almost stiff peaks then set aside.

In a larger bowl place the mix, water and yolks and beat on high for about 3 minutes. Add the melted chocolate and mix well. With a rubber spatula, carefully fold the egg whites in until fully incorporated.

Fill cupcake papers 2/3 full and bake in the center of the oven for about 18 minutes. Cupcakes are done when they spring back or when a tester inserted in the middle of the cupcake comes out clean.
Since cupcakes can dry out easily due to their size, never over bake. Remove from oven, allow to cool for no more than 3-5 minutes, the carefully remove from the pan and place on a cooling rack. The longer they remain in the hot pan the more they will continue to bake risking dry cupcakes. When cool, top with Coconut, Pecan Caramel Icing.

NOTE: If you prefer a more traditional presentation, divide batter into 3 8 inch cake pans that have been greased, dusted with coco powder and lined with parchment paper. Bake until tester comes out clean, approximately 20 minutes, cool on racks, transfer 1 layer at a time to a cake plate and ice tops only.

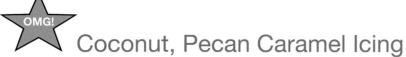

Coconut, Pecan Caramel Icing

German Chocolate cake could never be complete without it's traditional coconut pecan icing! While I have made the traditional recipe and substituted evaporated goat's milk with good results, this version is completely dairy free, and sugar free and like the cupcakes, it could not be easier to make! My daughter Angela, who follows a vegan lifestyle, inspired me to create this version and it is both fantastic and a much healthier version!

1 cup brown rice syrup
1 cup Thai Kitchen organic coconut milk
1/2 cup coconut butter
2 tablespoons coconut oil
1 teaspoons black strap molasses
1 cup chopped pecans
1 1/2 cups organic unsweetened coconut flakes
1 teaspoons vanilla extract

In a small pan over medium high heat, bring the brown rice syrup, coconut milk, coconut butter, coconut oil and molasses to a rolling boil for 5 minutes. Remove from heat and add pecans, coconut and vanilla. Cool to room temperature before icing cupcakes

Deep Chocolate Ganache

This is a dark, decadent, rich and smooth chocolate sauce that is versatile enough to ice cookies or cakes, but when warm it is also wonderful sauce for pound cake, ice cream or yogurt parfaits. It keeps well in the refrigerator so make a little extra and a special dessert is never more than a few moments away.
Yield – 1 cup

1 10 ounce package Tropical Source chocolate chips
1 tablespoon raw cacao powder
1 tablespoon coconut oil
1/4 cup unsweetened almond, soy or rice milk
1/2 teaspoon good quality vanilla extract

In a small sauce pan heat milk, cocoa powder and coconut oil until very warm. Remove from heat and add chocolate chips, stirring until smooth. If you would like a thinner sauce, add more warm milk, 1 tablespoon at a time, stirring until smooth after each addition until you achieve your desired consistency.

Raspberry and Lemon Crème Cupcakes

Refreshing and elegant, this is a dessert for a fancy tea, brunch or as mini-birthday cakes. These are light and airy from the beaten egg whites, tangy from the lemon and sour crème and perfectly moist from the fruit.
Yield – 1 dozen

1/2 cup room temperature butter
3/4 cup organic palm or cane sugar
1/4 teaspoon stevia
2 room temperature eggs, separated.
1 tablespoon lemon juice
1 1/2 teaspoon lemon zest
1 cup Sour Crème Substitute
1 3/4 cups spelt flour
1/2 teaspoon baking soda
1/4 teaspoon baking powder
1/4 teaspoon salt
1 cup fresh or frozen, defrosted and drained raspberries

Preheat oven to 350 degrees. Line muffin tin with cupcake papers.

In a small mixing bowl beat the egg whites until they form stiff peaks. Set aside.

In a large mixing bowl cream butter, stevia and sugar until very light and fluffy. Add eggs one at a time beating well after each addition. Add lemon juice, zest and sour crème substitute and beat at high speed for about 2 minutes.

Sift together the dry ingredients. Reduce speed to low and add slowly, mixing until well incorporated, scraping down the sides several times. The batter should be smooth and free of lumps. Gently fold in berries and egg whites. Fill each cupcake paper 3/4 full and bake in the center of the oven approximately 20-25 minutes or until tester is clean when inserted in the center cupcake. Cool in pan on a wire rack 5-10 minutes before removing from pan to complete cooling process.

Ice with Raspberry-Lemon Crème Icing and top with fresh raspberries and lemon zest.

Raspberry-Lemon Crème Icing

A wonderful take off on cream cheese icing . . . it is a pretty pink, slightly tart and creamy icing that you will love!
Yield – 1 1/2 cups

3 ounces room temperature goat cheese
2 tablespoons room temperature butter
3 cups well sifted organic powdered sugar
2 teaspoons fine lemon zest
Freshly squeezed lemon juice
1 tablespoon chopped fresh or defrosted raspberries

Whip goat cheese and butter until light and fluffy, add raspberries, lemon zest and 2 teaspoons lemon juice. Whip until fully incorporated. On low speed add powdered sugar 1 cup at a time until smooth. Add additional lemon juice as needed to achieve proper consistency. Whip 4-5 more minutes scraping the sides of the bowl occasionally.

Chocolate Buttercrème Icing

Trust me on this one . . . this is an icing you HAVE to try! It tastes a bit like a decadent chocolate truffle, and while there is chocolate in this icing, there is no butter and no sugar!
Yield - 1 1/4 cups

1 cup jewel or garnet yam puree
3 tablespoons cacao powder
1/8 teaspoon powdered stevia
1/2 teaspoon vanilla extract
2 tablespoons pH 9.5 ionized water

In a VitaMix or other powerful blender blend yam puree, stevia and coffee until very smooth. Transfer to a mixing bowl and add cacao powder, vanilla and 1 tablespoon water. Beat on high speed until light and fluffy. If necessary continue adding water, 1 tablespoon at a time until you achieve the proper consistency. Since yams vary in moisture content and sweetness, taste and if your icing is not quite sweet enough add 1 teaspoon agave nectar. Spread or pipe atop your favorite cupcake.

Basic Spelt Pound Cake

A pound cake was traditionally made with a pound of each of four ingredients, flour, butter, eggs, and sugar but over time it has gone through many regional changes. So here is the basic recipe . . . it is such a rich, reliably moist, sturdy and versatile cake that's often sliced and topped with fresh berries, or fruit compotes, cut into thin layers and filled with dried fruit and whipped topping.
Yield – 10-12 servings

3/4 cup room temperature butter
1 1/4 cups sugar - date, maple or cane crystals
1/8 teaspoon stevia powder
6 room temperature eggs, separated
1 teaspoon baking powder
1 1/2 teaspoons vanilla
2 1/4 cups triple-sifted white spelt flour

Preheat the oven to 325 degrees. Butter a 9 x 5 inch loaf pan and place a piece of buttered parchment paper in the bottom of the pan and set aside.

Using an electric mixer with a paddle attachment, beat butter until light and fluffy, add 1 cup sugar and beat for 3-4 minutes. Add one egg yolk at a time and beat well after each addition.   Add vanilla and salt and beat well. Turning the mixer down to low add the flour 3/4 cup at a time, scraping the bowl after each addition. Do not overmix once the flour has been added, but be certain it is well incorporated. Beat egg whites and remaining sugar until stiff peaks form, fold into batter.

Spoon or pour batter into prepared loaf pan and bake in the center of the oven for about 80 minutes or until cake tester comes out clean from the center of the cake (I generally start checking after 1 hour). Remove from oven and cool in pan for 5-10 minutes before removing and cooling completely on a wire rack.

Basic GF Pound Cake

This GF version is everything you expect in a delicious pound cake . . . slightly dense, moist, and buttery. It's so versatile it can be used as the base for so many simply elegant desserts. Make it ahead of time so you will be ready for a quick dessert any time!
Yield – 10-12 servings

1 cup room temperature butter
1 1/4 cup Vanilla Sugar
4 room temperature eggs, separated
1 3/4 cups GF Pastry Flour Blend, triple sifted
1 1/4 teaspoons baking powder
1/2 cup rice, soy or Very Vanilla Almond Milk

Preheat the oven to 350 degrees. Butter a 9 x 5 inch loaf pan and line the bottom with buttered parchment paper.

Add baking powder to flour in final sifting to ensure they are fully incorporated.

Using a mixer with a paddle attachment beat butter on high until light and fluffy. Add 1/2 cup sugar and beat for about 2-3 minutes, scraping down the sides frequently. Add eggs yolks one at a time and beat very well, about 1 minute, after each addition. Using low speed, add half of the flour mixture and mix just until combined, add milk mix briefly then add the remaining flour mixture and mix until completely combined. Beat egg whites and remaining sugar until stiff peaks form. Carefully fold into batter.

Pour batter into loaf pan and bake in the center of the oven for approximately 30 minutes or until cake tester comes out clean when inserted in the center of the cake.

Cool in the pan on a wire rack for about 10 minutes before removing from pan and cooling completely.

Slice and serve alone or topped with fresh berries, fruit compote or lemon curd. Wrap and refrigerate up to 1 week or freeze for a quick dessert anytime.

GF Crumble Topping

This versatile topping is perfect for almost any fruit. It's buttery and tender with just a little crunch, reminiscent of short-bread cookies. Make it in double batches and store in the freezer for a quick, elegant dessert in minutes!
Yield – 1 1/2 cups

1 1/4 cup Mama's GF Almond Blend Flour
1/3 cup butter
1/3 cup vanilla sugar
1/8 teaspoon xanthan or guar gum
1/8 teaspoon Celtic sea salt

Combine dry ingredients in a bowl. Using a pastry blender cut butter into flour mixture until mixture forms small crumbles about the size of large peas. Refrigerate at least 20 minutes.

Sprinkle over fruit fillings and bake according to directions.

Strawberry Rhubarb Crumble

Growing up rhubarb commonly grew in our yards and gardens so we used it in sauces, pies and cakes. This recipe is an abbreviated combo of them all. It's lovely color, the creamy texture, the interesting play between sweet and tart flavors and the buttery topping makes this one a recipe to remember!
Serves 4-6

4 cups rhubarb sliced into 1/2 inch pieces
3 tablespoons agave nectar
1/8 teaspoon stevia powder
1/4 cup freshly squeezed orange juice
1 tablespoon orange zest
2 cups sliced strawberries
1 1/4 cups GF Crumble Topping

Preheat oven to 350 degrees.

Combine all ingredients and place in an 8 x 8 inch baking dish. Sprinkle Crumble Topping over fruit, distributing evenly.
Bake in the center of the oven until fruit is bubbly and topping is lightly browned around the edges of the dish.

Remove from oven and cool slightly before serving. I like to add a small scoop of Strawberry Gelato or your favorite vanilla
ice cream.

GF Cobbler Topping

Cobbler topping is a lot like a sweet scone baked over fruit. Like scones, the topping has a nice crumbly texture, it's
slightly sweet, but neutral enough to let the fruit be the real star of the show! Cobblers are one of the easiest and most
loved desserts, and a great way to make fruit into an elegant, yet homey dessert!
Yield – 1 1/2 cups

1/4 cup palm shortening
2 teaspoons nutritional yeast
1 teaspoon ground flax seeds
1/2 teaspoon salt
1/4 teaspoon xanthan gum
1 1/4 cups Mama's GF Almond Blend Flour
1/4 teaspoon baking soda
1 teaspoon baking powder
1/2 cup buttermilk substitute

In a medium bowl, whisk all dry ingredients together until fully incorporated. Using a pastry cutter, work the shortening in
until the mixture looks like very small peas. Add buttermilk substitute and stir with a fork, just until combined.

Drop by spoonfuls over prepared fruit and bake according to directions.

 GF Blackberry Cobbler

Blackberry Cobbler is one of the quintessential desserts of late summer! Sweet blackberries baked with a touch of lemon and a perfect cobbler top . . . this is perfection! When you consider that blackberries are loaded with fiber, antioxidants and even Omega 3 fatty acids, they are the perfect ending to any meal!
Serves 4

3 cups fresh or frozen and defrosted blackberries
1 1/2 teaspoons lemon juice
3/4 teaspoon lemon zest
1 teaspoon agave nectar
2 pinches stevia powder
3 teaspoons tapioca pearls
Cobbler Topping (half
1/2 teaspoon Lemon Sugar

Preheat oven to 375 degrees.

In a deep 6 inch baking dish toss berries, juice, zest, tapioca and sweeteners together until well combined.

Drop Cobbler topping on by spoonfuls, leaving a bit of space between each bit of dough to allow fruit to bubble up and topping to expand. Sprinkle with Lemon Sugar and bake approximately 30 minutes or until top is golden and filling is bubbly.

Remove from oven and cool slightly. Serve warm or cold.

 GF Crisp Topping

This is the crisp, sweet, oat filled topping you remember, but it's GF! Filled with nutritious and delicious oats, sweet spices, black strap molasses and dates, this crunchy topping is the perfect topping for apples, peaches, pears and so much more!

Make extra and store in your freezer so you can pull a dessert together in minutes!
Yield – 2 cups

1 cup GF rolled oats
1 cup GF Pastry Flour
8 dates, pitted and chopped
1 tablespoon black strap molasses
1 teaspoon ground cinnamon
1/8 teaspoon sea salt
1/3 cup room temperature butter or Ghee

Place flour, dates and molasses in a food processer and pulse until fully incorporated. Add oats, cinnamon, salt and butter, pulse until all ingredients form a crumbly topping. Sprinkle evenly over fruit and bake according to recipe directions

Chai Spiced Peaches with GF Crisp Topping and Coconut Crème

This is a fantastic way to present a delicious, simple to make and deceptively nutritious dessert. Make it from fresh ripe peaches or from frozen halves and top with a generous dollop of Coconut Cream and a dash of Chai Spices and everyone will be asking for more!
Serves 6

3 peaches peeled, pitted and halved
1/2 teaspoon Chai Spice Blend
6 tablespoons GF Crisp Topping
6 tablespoons Coconut Whipped Crème

Arrange peach halves in a baking dish cut side up. Sprinkle with ¼ teaspoon Chai Spice Blend, then fill centers with Crisp Topping. Bake at 350 for 30 minutes. Cool to room temperature.

Meanwhile mix remaining 1/4 teaspoon Chai Spice Blend into Coconut Whipped Crème.   To serve place peach half on a plate, top with a tablespoon of crème and a sprinkle of Chai Spice Blend.

Very Vanilla Almond Milk Pudding

This is a smooth, creamy, almost addictive non-dairy pudding. Serve warm or cold, with or without fruit. It can even be used as a base for ice crèmes or added to fruity ice pops. It is so yummy . . . and I've included 2 versions for your convenience.
Yield - 3 Cups

2 cups Very Vanilla Almond Milk
4 egg yolks
2 whole eggs
1 inch piece vanilla bean
6 pitted dates
1 teaspoon agar powder
1 tablespoon sweet almond oil
1 tsp xanthan or guar gum

Alternate Recipe

2 cups unsweetened almond milk
4 whole eggs
1 1/2 inch piece vanilla bean
1/2 tsp good quality vanilla
1 teaspoon agar powder
1 tablespoon sweet almond oil
1 tsp xanthan or guar gum
Choose from these options for sweetener:
8 dates, or 2/3 cup agave nectar, or 1/4 cup agave nectar + 1/4 tsp powdered stevia

If using dates as your sweetener, blend all ingredients, exept Xanthan Gum, until dates are completely incorporated. Pour mixture into a saucepan and cook, stirring constantly over medium-low heat until it is the consistency of thin custard. At this point it should coat the back of a spoon. Remove from heat and pour back into the VitaMix and start blending on low. Slowly add the Xanthan gum and continue to blend on high for about 1 minute.

Blending will add a bit of air to your pudding and create a lighter and creamier texture. Pour into individual serving bowls, cover and refrigerate.

Lemon Curd

Intensely lemony, tart, sweet and delicious, lemon curd is a wonderful staple for creating desserts, yogurt parfaits and crepe fillings. It is easy to make and worth the effort!
Yield – 2 cups

4 whole organic eggs
1/3 cup agave nectar
1 large pinch stevia powder
2/3 cup lemon juice
2 tablespoons lemon zest
1 teaspoon agar powder
1/8 teaspoon guar or xanthan gum
1/3 cup butter

Beat eggs very well and strain to be certain there are no large pieces of protein that can create lumps in your curd.

In a sauce pan blend eggs, agave, stevia, lemon juice, zest and agar together. Slowly heat and stir until mixture completely coats the back of a spoon. Remove from heat and add guar gum. Stir in butter. If you want a lighter, airier texture, blend with immersion blender 2 minutes to incorporate air.

Transfer to a glass jar with a tight fitting lid. Cool completely before tightly capping. Keeps 2-3 weeks in the refrigerator.

Nutrition Note: Lemons and limes are not only packed with Vitamin C, they also contain important flavonoids that have been shown to stop cell division in certain cancers, activate white blood cells, reduce the symptoms of both osteo and rheumatoid arthritis and act as a powerful antibiotic against certain bacteria.

Mojito Curd

I'm not certain who the genius was who decided to blend the flavors of lemon, lime, mint and rum but it was inspired! Now you can experience them in ice box pies, sorbets, gelatos, tarts, muffins, over waffles and much more . . .
Yield – 3 1/2 cups

5 whole eggs
1/2 cup each lime and lemon juice
2 teaspoons each lime and lemon zest
1/4 cup finely chopped mint leaves
1/3 cup agave nectar
1/8 teaspoon stevia powder
1 teaspoon agar powder
1/4 teaspoon guar or xanthan gum
2 tablespoons rum
3 tablespoons Citrus Compound Butter

Beat eggs and yolks very well and strain to be certain there are no large pieces of protein that can create lumps in your curd.

In a sauce pan blend eggs, agave, stevia, lemon and lime juice, mint, agar and zests together. Slowly heat and stir until mixture will completely coat the back of a spoon. Remove from heat and add guar gum and rum. Stir in butter. Using VitaMix or immersion blender, blend 2-3 minutes.

Transfer to a glass jar with a tight fitting lid. Cool completely before tightly capping.
Keeps up to 3 weeks in the refrigerator.

Crème Anglaise

This is a smooth, creamy, sugar free and non-dairy version of a French custard sauce – it's actually a thin pudding. It is often used as a dessert sauce but is sometimes the star of the dessert. It can be served either warm or cold and refrigerated it will keep for several days. Pour it over a bowl of fresh berries, Pound Cake or as the base for Very Vanilla Ice Crème.
Yield - 2 Cups

1 1/2 cups Very Vanilla Almond Milk
4 egg yolks
1 egg
1 inch piece vanilla bean
5 pitted dates
1 tablespoon butter or ghee

In a VitaMix or other powerful blender, blend all ingredients until dates are completely incorporated. Pour mixture into a saucepan and cook, stirring constantly over medium-low heat until it coats the back of a spoon. Remove from heat, pour into a bowl, cover and cool.

Quick Coconut Crème Anglaise

This vegan version requires no cooking! It is very "coconutty" delicious and keeps well for about a week in the refrigerator. So it's easy, quick, yummy and convenient to keep on hand for a quick dessert sauce! The secret ingredient is Chao Thai Coconut Cream Powder – it's easy to find on line if your grocer doesn't carry it.
Yield – 3 cups

1 can Thai Kitchen organic coconut milk
2/3 cup So Delicious organic unsweetened coconut milk
2 tablespoons agave nectar
1/8 teaspoon stevia powder
1/2 cup coconut cream powder or concentrate
1/4 teaspoon xanthan or guar gum
1/2 teaspoon coconut extract
1 pinch salt

Pour all ingredients into a medium sized mixing bowl and blend with an immersion blender until mixture is thick, smooth and creamy. Continue blending about 1 minute to incorporate more air into the mixture. That's all there is to it, it literally could not be easier!

 # Quick Caramel Sauce

This is the easiest, most nutritious sweet sauce you will ever eat. Brown rice syrup and black strap molasses are both examples of nutrient dense sweeteners. This 2 ingredient sauce takes advantage of them both to create a thick, rich sauce that tastes buttery and takes literally 5 minutes to make from start to finish!
Yield - 1/2 cup

1/2 cup organic brown rice syrup
1/2 teaspoon black strap molasses

Place in a small saucepan over medium heat. Stirring constantly, cook just until bubbles form around the edges of the pan and the color darkens slightly (in areas with higher humidity bring to a rolling boil for 2 minutes). Remove from heat and cool slightly before serving. This sauce does not require refrigeration.

Raspberry Sauce

This beautiful jewel toned sauce is a fruity, sweet and smooth topping for ice crèmes, Pound Cakes, a filling for layer cakes or to swirl in Deep Chocolate Mousse Gelato, Mascarpone Substitute or your morning yogurt.
Yield – 1 cup

1 1/2 cups fresh or frozen raspberries crushed
1 tablespoon agave
Pinch stevia powder
1 teaspoon orange zest

In a small sauce pan, over low heat, cook berries and agave until the juices are running. Run about half of the cooked berries through a sieve to remove the seeds, add pulp and zest into pan. Stir to incorporate, pour into a bowl, cover and refrigerate until completely cooled.

Kitchen Tip: Transforming a simple cake or scoop of ice creme into an elegant dessert is as simple as adding a delicious sauce and a sprinkle of chocolate shavings, chopped nuts or a few fresh berries . . . leaving everyone to wonder if you have secretly been training as a pastry chef!

GF Lemon Cookie Crust

Now that's a lemon crust! . . . are words you will hear over and over when your family and friends taste this crust. It is so delicious and easy to prepare because it uses Pamela's GF Lemon Shortbread.
Yield – 1 pie crust

1 3/4 cup Pamela's GF Lemon Shortbread cookie crumbs
1/3 cup very soft, room temperature butter
Pinch Celtic sea salt

Process cookies in a food processor until cookies become evenly sized crumbs. Add salt and butter then pulse a few times to distribute evenly. Press crumbs into bottom and sides of an 8 – 9 inch pie plate. Freeze 1 hour or bake at 350 degrees for 15 minutes, cool on rack before filling.

 # GF Chocolate-Almond Crust

I decided that some of my desserts deserved a chocolate tart crust. But I wanted it to be no-fuss and simple to assemble, but I also wanted it to have a rich taste with a bit of crunch, so here it is!
Yield – 1 6-8 inch tart shell

1/2 cup almonds
1 tablespoon almond butter
1 tablespoon coconut butter
1 tablespoon coconut oil
1 1/2 cups GF rolled oats
1 tablespoon cocoa powder
1 tablespoon palm sugar
1-2 teaspoons pH 9.5 ionized water

In a food processor fitted with a metal blade, process the nuts and oatmeal until medium-fine. Add remaining ingredients and process until the texture of moist crumbs. Press dough into the bottom and sides of a 7-8 inch tart pan that has been sprayed with coconut oil. Bake at 350 for about 20 minutes. Cool completely before filling.

GF Rustic Oat Crust and Topping

This crumble style crust is so delicious that you will be lucky to get it into the tart pan before it's gone! It tastes almost like a delicious oatmeal cookie. It is the perfect sweet and crunchy compliment to tart stone fruit. So whatever the season, choose the fruit that is in abundance and be certain fill one of these tart shells. (Photo page 219)
Yield – 1 8 inch tart shell

1 1/2 cups GF rolled oats
10 dates
1 tablespoon coconut cream
1 tablespoon coconut oil
1 tablespoon butter

In a food processor, blend the ingredients until they turn into a moist crumble. Press crumbles into a tart pan that has been sprayed with coconut oil. Reserve remaining crumbles as a topping. Bake at 350 for 10 minutes to slightly set the crust. Add filling, top with remaining crumbles and bake until golden brown.

If filling with gelato, ice crème or pudding, the crust is delicious raw. Simply press into oiled tart pan and freeze for at least 1 hour before filling. It's a little trickier to get the first piece out, but totally worth the effort.

Chocolate and Salted Caramel Tartlets with Toasted Pecans

These little treats are heavenly little bites and surprisingly enough they are actually a treat that treats your body well! They are made with dark chocolate, filled with powerful antioxidants, chewy, creamy caramel made from mineral dense brown rice syrup and pecans that are power packed bits of protein, fiber, essential fatty acids and minerals. So the next time you are feeling the call of chocolate, here's your answer! If you have Quick Caramel Sauce and Deep Chocolate Ganache on hand this will literally take seconds to assemble. If not, it's still a quick chocolate fix! (Photo page 196)
Yield – 4 mini tarts

GF Scottish Shortbread Cookie Dough
1/2 cup toasted pecans roughly chopped
1/2 cup Quick Caramel Sauce
3/4 cup Deep Chocolate Ganache
1/4 teaspoon flake sea salt

Press shortbread dough into tart pan bottoms and sides to provide an even, yet slightly thin crust. Bake at 325 degrees for about 20 minutes. Cool and leave in pans until tart fillings have completely set.

Divide chopped pecans evenly among tart shells. Place caramel sauce in a small sauce pan and boil 2 minutes. Pour half over pecans. Meanwhile heat ganache in a double boiler until it's smooth and stirable. Pour over caramel layer.

Return caramel to heat and boil until a hardened stream forms when you lift a spoon out of the pan. Quickly form spiral shapes on parchment paper and cool. Top tart with hard caramel spiral and a sprinkle of flaked or coarse sea salt. Cool completely, cut each tart into 4-6 wedges and serve with an espresso, latte or a cup of tea.

 # Raspberry Truffle Tart

This little tart is so delicate and decadent . . . rich dark chocolate, slightly tart raspberry sauce and sweet fresh raspberries. It's pretty as a picture and a sweet ending to any meal.
Yield - 8 inch tart

GF Double Chocolate Shortbread Cookie Dough
1/3 cup Deep Chocolate Ganache
1/3 cup Raspberry Sauce
1/2 cup fresh raspberries

Preheat oven to 350 degrees.

Press enough shortbread dough into tart pan to create an even crust, bake until set and slightly crisp around edges, about 25 minutes. Remove from oven and cool completely.

Cover bottom of the tart shell with ganache, top with raspberry sauce and fresh raspberries.

Set aside for about 30 minutes or until ganache has set. Serve room temperature.

GF Very Berry Mojito Pie

This is such a refreshing ice box pie, and not one you are likely to find outside your own kitchen. The complex flavors of a Mojito combined with the creaminess of mascarpone and the fresh sweetness of fresh berries . . . this one is a must to try. It's such an intensely flavored pie that a small piece is satisfying.
Yield – 8-10 pieces

1 GF Lemon Cookie Crumb Crust
1 1/2 cups Mojito Curd
2 cups Mascarpone Substitute
1 tablespoon dark rum (optional)
2 cups mixed fresh berries
1 teaspoon lemon or lime zest
Mint sprigs for garnish

Mix curd, mascarpone crème and rum. Fill cooled crust, top with fresh berries, zest and mint. Refrigerate at least 1 hour then serve and enjoy!

Fresh Figs with Chocolate Balsamic Reduction and Mascarpone

A young friend of mine once exclaimed that she thought figs were nature's candy, and I wholeheartedly agree! They are a nutrient dense fruit, high in potassium, calcium, magnesium, copper and manganese as well as fiber! Who could ask for more . . . delicious and nutritious! This simple preparation enhances their delicate nature without masking their unique flavor. Prepared in this way these fresh delicacies can be passed on a tray as an appetizer, enjoyed as a part of a fruit and cheese tray, be the star of an otherwise simple salad or stand alone as an elegant dessert. (Photo on page 84.)
Serves 4 as a dessert

8 fresh figs
2 tablespoons soft Mascarpone Substitute
2 teaspoons Chocolate Balsamic Vinegar
1/8 teaspoon freshly ground coarse black pepper

Gently rinse figs, pat dry and slice in half lengthwise. Fill pastry bag, fitted with a star tip, with room temperature Mascarpone Substitute. There will be a natural indention in the center of the fig. Drizzle vinegar over figs, filling the center indention, pipe cheese over the indention. Lightly sprinkle with pepper and serve.

Deep Chocolate Mousse Gelato

Dark, rich chocolate that is so velvety and satisfying you will be instantly hooked! It is so amazing as it is, but let your imagination be your guide in adding delicious toppings. This is a perfect gelato and the fact that it's non-dairy is a bonus!
Yield – 2 1/2 cups

1 package organic silken tofu
10 ounces Tropical Source chocolate chips
1 tablespoon raw cacao powder
1 tablespoon agave
1/2 teaspoon vanilla
1 pinch Celtic sea salt
1 teaspoon guar or xanthan gum

Line a mesh colander with a double layer of coffee filters or a triple layer of cheesecloth. Open the box of tofu and carefully transfer to colander to drain for approximately 1 hour. Draining the tofu keeps any ice crystals from forming during freezing.
Melt chocolate chips in a double boiler. Be certain to keep the heat low and remove from heat when about half of the chocolate is melted. Add cacao, agave and vanilla. Stir until chocolate is smooth.

Place tofu, chocolate chip mixture, salt and guar gum in VitaMix, blend until smooth.

Transfer to a covered bowl and chill in freezer until it begins to freeze around the outside of the container. Spoon into the bowl of your ice cream freezer and freeze according to manufacturer's directions. This mixture is so thick that it requires a bit of stirring to it moving so it will freeze evenly. I use a spatula to keep it churning along.

Deep Chocolate Mousse and Raspberry Swirl Gelato

A swirl of a raspberry sauce adds a delicious dimension to this velvety gelato.
Once gelato is frozen, stir in 1/2 cup Raspberry Sauce and 1/4 cup Chocolate Sauce. Return to the freezer until ready to serve. Scoop into bowls and garnish with a few fresh raspberries and a drizzle of chocolate sauce.

Lemon Ricotta Gelato with Pistachios and Tart Cherries

This is one of my very favorite ice creams. It is that ideal combination of a perfectly creamy texture, tart, lemony flavor, studded with little jewels of crunchy pistachios and chewy sweet-tart cherries. All of this and it takes only 15 minutes to freeze if you have already stocked your refrigerator with easy to make Ricotta Substitute and Lemon Curd! It's an ice cream that feels wonderfully decadent, but is actually a light, healthy frozen treat you can feel good about eating.
Yield – 1 quart

2 1/2 cups Ricotta Substitute
1 cup Lemon Curd
1/4 cup pistachios, roughly chopped
1/4 cup dried tart cherries, roughly chopped

Mix together until thoroughly blended, spoon into ice cream freezer bowl and process according to manufacturer's directions.

This is so thick already that you will need to move it from the center to the outside of your container a few times during the freezing process. If your curd and cheese is already cold it will take only about 15 minutes to complete the freezing process.

Scoop directly into serving bowls or into a container and place in the freezer until you are ready to serve.

Very Vanilla Gelato

This is very rich, very creamy and very vanilla . . . serve alone or atop warm Peach and Blackberry Cobbler, Pound Cake and berries, Apple Crisp, Pear Torte or atop any bowl of fresh berries. Just like traditional vanilla ice cream, it is so versatile you will want to keep some on hand in your freezer.
Yield – 1 quart

3 cups Very Vanilla Almond Pudding
1 cup Sweet Almond Crème
Seeds and paste from 1 inch piece vanilla pod

Mix well and chill in freezer until very cold. Add to ice cream maker and process according to manufacturer's directions.
Scoop into bowls and top with your favorite toppings.

Nutty Coconut Ice Crème

This is a truly delicious ice cream that is
very close to my absolute favorite BR flavor, Gone Nutty Coconut. It's super easy
to make, uses only a few ingredients, is
sweetened with agave and stevia for a
low glycemic index, and is packed with
toasted coconut and nuts . . . what's not
to love about this cold and creamy treat?
Yield – 3 1/2 cups

3 cups Quick Vegan Coconutty Crème
Anglaise
1 teaspoon coconut extract
1/2 cup toasted nuts
2 tablespoons toasted coconut flakes

Mix coconut extract and Coconutty
Crème Anglaise and process in ice
cream freezer according to the manufacturer's instructions. During the last 5
minutes add toasted coconut and nuts.
Serve immediately or store in freezer
until ready to scoop.

Peach Praline Semifreddo

Semifreddo is a delicious frozen dessert that doesn't require any special equipment, but looks like it came from a high end pastry shop. It's one of the most beautiful desserts you can serve and deceptively easy to make. Traditionally it is filled with sugar and heavy cream, but this one is made with brown rice syrup, creamy Mascarpone Substitute and light as air meringue folded together and frozen in a loaf pan. What a terrific way to beat the summer heat! (Photo front cover)
Yield – 6 slices

1 1/2 cups Mascarpone Substitute at room temperature
3 eggs, separated
1/3 cup honey or agave nectar
1 teaspoon Peach Balsamic Vinegar (optional but really yummy)
1/2 teaspoon good quality vanilla extract
1/2 cup Pecan Pralines chopped finely
6 Pecan Pralines in 2 inch circles
12 pecan halves coated in praline syrup
5 ripe peaches

Place egg whites and 2 tablespoons sweetener in a stainless steel bowl over simmering water. Using a whisk or an electric hand mixer beat the egg whites until soft peaks form and they reach 140 degrees. Set aside while you beat the yolks.*

Place egg yolks and sweetener in a stainless steel bowl over simmering water. With a whisk or an electric hand mixer beat until they are light and lemon in color and they reach 140 degrees.

Peel and pit 2 peaches and puree. Add room temperature Mascarpone Substitute, vanilla extract and Peach Balsamic Vinegar and blend thoroughly. Pour into yolks and fold in until completely incorporated.

Peel, pit and dice 2 additional peaches. Fold in peaches and 1/4 cup chopped pralines. Now very carefully fold in the egg whites to ensure that they are not deflated. Pour into a lightly buttered loaf pan and place in freezer for about 3 hours. For easy removal place loaf pan in a hot water bath for 30 seconds to 1 minute then invert onto serving tray. Sprinkle chopped pralines around all sides of the semifreddo, leaving the top unadorned. Slice remaining peach and arrange on top of the loaf alternating with whole pralines and pecan halves. Slice with a knife dipped in hot water and serve!

*Note: Organic, fresh eggs from a trusted source can be used without heating, otherwise they should be heated to pasteurize them.

Pecan Pralines

This is a super healthy, crunchy, and absolutely delicious nutty candy treat! And there are only 3 ingredients! Let the brown rice syrup do its magic and make you look like an accomplished pastry chef and candy maker! These make a beautiful gift stacked in a glass cylinder. I use them to decorate cakes, cupcakes and frozen treats.

Yield - Approximately 2 dozen 2-3 inch candies

1 1/2 cups brown rice syrup
1 teaspoon black strap molasses
1 1/2 cups pecan halves
1 teaspoon good quality vanilla

Lightly toast the pecans. Bring brown rice syrup to a boil for about 2 minutes. Test by dropping a teaspoon onto parchment paper. It should set up immediately. Retest every minute until consistency is achieved. If humidity is a bit high this can take up to 8 minutes.

Remove from heat, add vanilla and pecans and stir until pecans are evenly coated.

Working very quickly, spoon out into 3 inch rounds on buttered parchment paper. Cool completely before popping off the paper. Store in a tightly covered glass bowl or tin lined in parchment paper.

If the humidity is a bit high, they can get a little sticky. If this happens, place back on parchment paper and put into your oven set on the lowest setting for about 30 minutes, turn the oven off and cool in the oven.

When making the pralines for Peach Praline Semifreddo, coat about a dozen pecan halves and drop them on the buttered parchment paper to use as garnish along with the pralines.

Recipe Index

Key Word Index